Practical Responsive Typography

Get your attractive type design up and running in the browser with real-world, responsive, and tailored tutorials

Dario Calonaci

[PACKT] open source✲
community experience distilled
PUBLISHING

BIRMINGHAM - MUMBAI

Practical Responsive Typography

First published: July 2016

Production reference: 2260716

Published by Packt Publishing Ltd.
Livery Place
35 Livery Street
Birmingham B3 2PB, UK.

ISBN 978-1-78588-463-4

www.packtpub.com

Credits

Author
Dario Calonaci

Reviewer
Chen Hui Jing

Commissioning Editor
Amarabha Banerjee

Acquisition Editor
Tushar Gupta

Content Development Editor
Mamata Walkar

Technical Editor
Nirant Carvalho

Copy Editors
Safis Editing
Madhusudan Uchil

Project Coordinator
Shweta H Birwatkar

Proofreader
Safis Editing

Indexer
Pratik Shirodkar

Graphics
Kirk D'Penha

Production Coordinator
Arvindkumar Gupta

Cover Work
Arvindkumar Gupta

About the Author

Dario Calonaci is a published author, correspondent, and professional advisor as well as design writer and reviewer for many publications, both print and online. Having worked on projects for The Ritz-Carlton and on Obama for America '12, The United Nations Rio+20 Conference, he's a well-known expert in the field of typography, which made him start teaching that and web design in his early twenties! As a member of various international groups, his art has been published worldwide in a plethora of books and magazines, from Phadon to Zeixs, and has been exposed in many openings, from New York's Times Square to the Senate Library in Rome.

He runs his own design firm at Kerned Studio in Florence for clients such as Gucci, Calvin Klein, and Berni among many others. You can take a look at his work on www.kernedstudio.com and www.dariocalonaci.com.

About the Reviewer

Chen Hui Jing is a self-taught designer and developer from Singapore. Reducing the lines of code in her web projects makes her extremely happy. She used to play basketball full time and launched her web career during downtime between training sessions.

As a strong believer of HTML and CSS being the foundation of the Web, and she started Talk.CSS, the first CSS-centric meetup in Singapore, to encourage developers to further their understanding of CSS and how it can improve our designs on the Web.

www.PacktPub.com

eBooks, discount offers, and more

Did you know that Packt offers eBook versions of every book published, with PDF and ePub files available? You can upgrade to the eBook version at www.PacktPub.com and as a print book customer, you are entitled to a discount on the eBook copy. Get in touch with us at customercare@packtpub.com for more details.

At www.PacktPub.com, you can also read a collection of free technical articles, sign up for a range of free newsletters and receive exclusive discounts and offers on Packt books and eBooks.

https://www2.packtpub.com/books/subscription/packtlib

Do you need instant solutions to your IT questions? PacktLib is Packt's online digital book library. Here, you can search, access, and read Packt's entire library of books.

Why subscribe?

- Fully searchable across every book published by Packt
- Copy and paste, print, and bookmark content
- On demand and accessible via a web browser

Table of Contents

Preface

This book will take your typography knowledge from starter level to pro, focusing on clear writing, simple real-world examples, and the application of both of these to the exciting World Wide Web!

Typography is one of the most important parts of any website's design. This book will show you, with practical examples, how you can implement practical typography techniques to make your site responsive. This book will be a mix of responsive typography concepts and its practical implementations. The best way to approach this topic is to give users a clear roadmap to the fundamental ways of responsive typography, scaling and optimizing screen spaces, using Web Fonts and the multiple ways to do so, and the common pitfalls in this process. Then, the book will move towards real hands-on examples that will make you design your own responsive typography designs and customize existing designs without any external help.

What this book covers

Chapter 1, *Web Typography*, introduces you to all the basic knowledge about typography.

Chapter 2, *Responsive Typography*, explains the basic application of the general knowledge of typography — applied on the Web.

Chapter 3, *Web Fonts and Services*, provides an overhauled look at the different solutions for custom fonts on the Web.

Chapter 4, *Modern Scale*, is an introduction to typography scales — and how to apply them.

Chapter 5, *Viewport and Size*, provides an introduction to viewport area and units — and, again, how to use them.

Chapter 6, Media Queries, explains what media queries are—and, of course, how to use them.

Chapter 7, Sass and Typography, is an introduction to Sass, what it is, and how it can help you write better CSS, along with a lot of examples of using it for better typography.

Chapter 8, Three Step Responsive, is a follow-up to the previous chapters, summarizing all the previous information and explaining how to apply it to your website's typography.

Chapter 9, Future Responsive – Hinting, takes a quick look at hinting, what it is, and an example solution to what will likely come in the future.

Chapter 10, Future Responsive – Drop Caps and Shapes, provides a quick look at the future of Web typography, with the introduction of drop caps and shapes on the Web—and how to code them now.

What you need for this book

You only need a code editor, Koala or any Sass-processing software, and a web browser.

Who this book is for

This book is for web developers who are familiar with the basics of HTML5 and CSS3 and want to learn how to implement responsive typography efficiently and effectively. However, you do not require any coding experience to make full use of this book.

Conventions

In this book, you will find a number of text styles that distinguish between different kinds of information. Here are some examples of these styles and an explanation of their meaning.

Code words in text, database table names, folder names, filenames, file extensions, pathnames, dummy URLs, user input, and Twitter handles are shown as follows: "It's time to add some CSS properties to the preceding <p>."

A block of code is set as follows:

```
<h1>Nothing but Death</h1>
<h2>Pablo Neruda - 1926</h2>
<p> There are cemeteries that are lonely[…]</p>
```

New terms and **important words** are shown in bold. Words that you see on the screen, for example, in menus or dialog boxes, appear in the text like this: "You'll just have to click that **Publish** button from time to time and that's it."

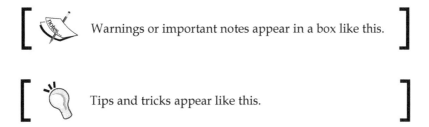

Warnings or important notes appear in a box like this.

Tips and tricks appear like this.

Reader feedback

Feedback from our readers is always welcome. Let us know what you think about this book—what you liked or disliked. Reader feedback is important for us as it helps us develop titles that you will really get the most out of.

To send us general feedback, simply e-mail feedback@packtpub.com, and mention the book's title in the subject of your message.

If there is a topic that you have expertise in and you are interested in either writing or contributing to a book, see our author guide at www.packtpub.com/authors.

Customer support

Now that you are the proud owner of a Packt book, we have a number of things to help you to get the most from your purchase.

Downloading the example code

You can download the example code files for this book from your account at http://www.packtpub.com. If you purchased this book elsewhere, you can visit http://www.packtpub.com/support and register to have the files e-mailed directly to you.

You can download the code files by following these steps:

1. Log in or register to our website using your e-mail address and password.
2. Hover the mouse pointer on the **SUPPORT** tab at the top.
3. Click on **Code Downloads & Errata**.
4. Enter the name of the book in the **Search** box.
5. Select the book for which you're looking to download the code files.
6. Choose from the drop-down menu where you purchased this book from.
7. Click on **Code Download**.

You can also download the code files by clicking on the **Code Files** button on the book's webpage at the Packt Publishing website. This page can be accessed by entering the book's name in the **Search** box. Please note that you need to be logged in to your Packt account.

Once the file is downloaded, please make sure that you unzip or extract the folder using the latest version of:

- WinRAR / 7-Zip for Windows
- Zipeg / iZip / UnRarX for Mac
- 7-Zip / PeaZip for Linux

The code bundle for the book is also hosted on GitHub at `https://github.com/PacktPublishing/Practical-Responsive-Typography`. We also have other code bundles from our rich catalog of books and videos available at `https://github.com/PacktPublishing/`. Check them out!

Errata

Although we have taken every care to ensure the accuracy of our content, mistakes do happen. If you find a mistake in one of our books — maybe a mistake in the text or the code — we would be grateful if you could report this to us. By doing so, you can save other readers from frustration and help us improve subsequent versions of this book. If you find any errata, please report them by visiting `http://www.packtpub.com/submit-errata`, selecting your book, clicking on the **Errata Submission Form** link, and entering the details of your errata. Once your errata are verified, your submission will be accepted and the errata will be uploaded to our website or added to any list of existing errata under the Errata section of that title.

To view the previously submitted errata, go to `https://www.packtpub.com/books/content/support` and enter the name of the book in the search field. The required information will appear under the **Errata** section.

Piracy

Piracy of copyrighted material on the Internet is an ongoing problem across all media. At Packt, we take the protection of our copyright and licenses very seriously. If you come across any illegal copies of our works in any form on the Internet, please provide us with the location address or website name immediately so that we can pursue a remedy.

Please contact us at copyright@packtpub.com with a link to the suspected pirated material.

We appreciate your help in protecting our authors and our ability to bring you valuable content.

Questions

If you have a problem with any aspect of this book, you can contact us at questions@packtpub.com, and we will do our best to address the problem.

1
Web Typography

Hello! Wonder no more about typography, it's fascinating mysteries, sensual shapes, and everything else you wanted to know about it; this book is about to reveal everything on the subject for you! Typography forms the base of a good written communication—it's an art form in itself, the art of drawing with words. While speaking you set the mood with tone and gesture, with writing nothing is more important than the words themselves and how they are portrayed.

Every letter, every curve, and every shape in the written form conveys feelings; so it's important to learn everything about it if you want to be a better designer.

You also need to know how readable your text is, therefore you have to set it up following some natural constraints our eyes and minds have built in, how white space influences your message, how every form should be taken into consideration in the writing of a text and this book will tell you exactly that!

Plus a little more!

You will also learn how to approach all of the above in today number one medium, the World Wide Web. Since 95 percent of the Web is made of typography, according to Oliver Reichenstein, it's only logical that if you want to approach the Web you surely need to understand it better.

Through this first chapter, you'll learn all the basics of typography and will be introduced to it core features, such as:

- Anatomy
- Line height
- Families
- Kerning

Note that typography, the art of drawing with words, is really ancient, as much as 3200 years prior to the appearance of Christ and the very first book on this matter is the splendid *Manuale Tipografico* from Giambattista Bodoni, which he self-published in 1818. Taking into consideration all the old data, and the new knowledge, everything started from back then and every rule that has been born in print is still valid today, even for the different medium that the Web is.

Developing your knowledge

From now on, I will be guiding you within the beautiful world that a word is and how it is expressed visually. You won't need anything more than your curiosity and an open and receptive mind.

No software, no technology unless you're reading this book on a screen and even in that case, you're ready to go!

How good is that!

Anatomy of the character

In this section, you will learn the terminology and structure of a letter. Knowing the what and where will make you a better writer and more importantly, a better reader. You'll start recognizing other people's mistakes, the world is full of them

The following points are the real foundation of writing, what lies beneath the splendid coherent surface of a text:

- Apexes are the points at the top of a character where the left and right strokes meet.

- **Arms** and **legs** are short strokes that extend from the main body, in all directions. The arms point upwards while legs are attached to the bottom, both of them are present on a lowercase k.

- **Ascenders** are truly important to the text and are segments that extend past the lowercase character x-height. They are clearly visible in b, d, f, h, k, l, and t.

- **Bars** are segments connecting the left and right portion of a character. A, H, R, and f have them and they rarely extend past the body.

- The **baseline** is the line where the character stands, and as an optical correction letter curves often extend pas it, to visually balance the height.

- **Bowls** are curved strokes that define a space within the body.

- **Cap height** addresses the measure of capitals, from baseline to top. Its better to measure them starting from a very flat bottom.

- **Counters** are the sections of space, semi or completely enclosed, within the body of the character.

- **Descenders** are the part of a character that descend below the baseline, as the g bowl for example.

- The **ear** is a small stroke visible on lowercase g, extending on the right of the bowl. They are not merely a decoration, they help with tracking and readability.

- **Finials** are curved ends, such as the ones in some lowercase e.

- **Hairline** is a section in the middle of some serif characters where the stroke is relatively thinner.

- **Links** are the little strokes that connect the top and bottom bowls of some fonts of g, such as Times New Roman.

- **Loops** are the bottom bowls of some font styles of g.

- **Serifs** are the endings, non-structural decoration present on some typefaces. They can be bracketed with a supportive curved connection or un-bracketed, whereby a straight connection is made at ninety degrees.

- **Shoulders** are the curved strokes that are attached to the stem.

- The **spine** is the main curved stroke of the S.

- The **Spurs** are small projections of the curve in capital G.

- **Stems** are the main, vertical, or diagonal strokes in a character; basically, the main foundation.

- **Strokes**, which we referred to previously, are nothing more than a curved or straight segment in a letter.

- **Swashes** are flourishes or decorations that sometimes replace serifs.

- **Tails** are descending strokes of R or Q.

- The **terminals** are the end of the stroke that is not terminating with a serif, such as the upper one of the small f.

- **X-height** is the main referred height in every typeface, especially for the lowercase x because of the flat bottom and upper area without ascenders or descenders.

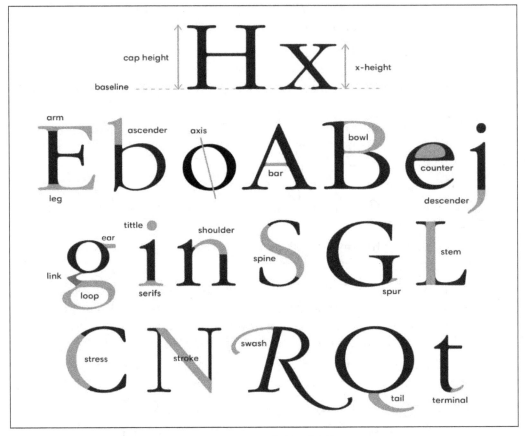

Image courtesy - TheTypeStudio

Typeface or font? A guide to the distinction

After seeing each character on its own, lets look at the bigger picture:

- **Typeface**: A typeface is a set of symbols, numbers, or letters that define the family.
- **Font**: A font on the other hand is the complete character set within a style and a particular weight of that typeface.

Typefaces are made of multiple fonts, which are made of multiple characters.

As of today, whereas type is laid principally on screens and not on paper, this distinction practically merged the two terms into the generic font one. Old printing and typesetting machines used letters carved out of metal imposed on woodblocks that needed to be covered in ink and then pushed on paper, leaving a trace. For this reason, each letter was unique and had to be made from scratch, for each weight and style within the same typeface. While your font may have 512 glyphs that weigh a certain kilobytes, the original handmade version had 512 physical blocks, (one for each letter), that weighed kilos. Therefore, with so many objects around that needed to be ordered in some way and so the division between style set and the complete typeface was born.

In addition, the same story of moving blocks gave birth to almost every other typography related terminology that we use today, even in the digital age. They will be addressed later in this topic.

Typefaces classification

The most commonly used type classification is based on the technical style and as such it's the one we are going to analyze and use. They are as follows:

Serifs

Serifs are referred to as such because of the small details that extend from the ending shapes of the characters; the origin of the word itself is obscure, various explanations have been given but none has been accepted as resolute.

Their origin can be traced back to the Latin alphabets of Roman times, probably because of the flares of the brush marks in corners, which were later chiseled in stone by the carvers.

They generally give better readability in print than on a screen, probably because of the better definition and evolution of the former in hundreds of years, while the latter technology is, on an evolutionary path, a newborn.

With the latest technologies and the high definition monitors that can rival the print definition, multiple scientific studies have been found inconclusive, showing that there is no discernible difference in readability between sans and serifs on the screen and as of today they are both used on the Web.

Within this general definition, there are multiples sub-families, as Old Style or Humanist.

Old Style or Humanist

The oldest ones, dating as far back as the mid 1400s are recognized for the diagonal guide on which the characters are built on; these are clearly visible for example on the **e** and **o** of **Adobe Jenson**.

Adobe Jenson

Transitional Serifs

They are neither antique nor modern and they date back to the 1700s and are generally numerous.

They tend to abandon some of the diagonal stress, but not all of them, especially keeping the **o**. **Georgia** and **Baskerville** are some well-known examples.

Baskerville

Modern Serifs

Modern Serifs tend to rely on the contrast between thick and thin strokes, abandon diagonal for vertical stress, and on more straight serifs. They appeared in the late 1700s.

Bodoni and Didot are certainly the most famous typefaces in this family.

Slab Serifs

Slab Serifs have little to no contrast between strokes, thick serifs, and sometimes appear with fixed widths, the underlying base resembles one of the sans more.

American Typewriter is the most famous typefaces in this family as shown in the following image:

American Typewriter

Sans Serifs

They are named so due to the loss of the decorative serifs, in French "sans" stands for "without". Sans Serif is a more recent invention, since it was born in the late 18th century.

They are divided into the following four sub-families:

Grotesque Sans

It is the earliest of the bunch; its appearance is similar to the serif with contrasted strokes but without serifs and with angled terminals

Franklin Gothic is one of the most famous typefaces in this family.

Franklin Gothic

Neo-Grotesque Sans

It is plain looking with little to no contrast, small apertures, and horizontal terminals. They are one of the most common font styles ranging from Arial and Helvetica to Universe.

Helvetica

Humanist font

They have a friendly tone due to the calligraphic style with a mixture of different widths characters and, most of the times, contrasted strokes.

Gill Sans being the flag-carrier.

Gill Sans

Geometric font

Based on the geometric and rigorous shapes, they are more modern and are used less for body copy. They have a general simplicity but readability of their characters is difficult.

Futura is certainly the most famous geometric font.

Futura

Script typefaces

They are usually classified into two sub-families based upon the handwriting, with cursive aspect and connected letterforms. They are as follows:

- Formal script
- Casual script
- Monospaced typefaces
- Display typefaces

Formal script

They are reminiscent of the handwritten letterforms common in the 17th and 18th centuries, sometimes they are also based on handwritings of famous people.

They are commonly used for elevated and highly elegant designs and are certainly unusable for long body copy.

Kunstler Script is a relatively recent formal script.

Casual script

This is less precise and tends to resemble a more modern and fast handwriting. They are as recent as the mid-twentieth century.

Mistral is certainly the most famous casual script.

Monospaced typefaces

Almost all the aforementioned families are proportional in their style, (each character takes up space that is proportional to its width). This sub-family addresses each character width as the same, with narrower ones, such as **i**, just gain white space around them, sometimes resulting in weird appearances. Hence, Due to their nature and their spacing, they aren't advised as copy typefaces, since their mono spacing can bring unwanted visual imbalance to the text.

Courier is certainly the most known monospaced typeface.

Courier New

Display typefaces

They are the broadest category and are aimed at small copy to draw attention and rarely follow rules, spreading from every one of the preceding families and expressing every mood.

 Recently even Blackletters (the very first fonts designed with the very first, physical printing machines) are being named under this category.

For example, **Danube** and **Val** are just two of the multitude that are out there:

Expressing different moods

In conjunction with the division of typography families, it's also really important for every project, both in print and web, to know what they express and why.

It takes years of experience to understand those characteristics and the method to use them correctly; here we are just addressing a very basic distinction to help you start with.

Remember that in typography and type design, every curve conveys a different mood, so just be patient while studying and designing.

Serifs vs Sans

Serifs, through their decorations, their widths, and in and out of their every sub-family convey old and antique/traditional serious feelings, even when more modern ones are used; they certainly convey a more formal appearance.

On the other hand, sans serif are aimed at a more modern and up-to-date world, conveying technological advancement, rationality, usually but not always, and less of a human feeling. They're more mechanical and colder than a serif, unless the author voluntarily designed them to be more friendly than the standard ones..

Serious vs Informal

Times New Roman   Verdana

Scripts vs scripts

As said, they are of two types, and as the name suggests, the division is straightforward.

Vladimir is elegant, refined, upper class looking, and expresses feelings such as respect. Arizonia on the other hand is not completely informal but is still a schizophrenic mess of strokes and a conclusion less expression of feeling; I'm not sure whether I feel amused or offended for its exaggerated confidentiality.

I'm elegant vs I'm a mess

Vladimir Script   Arizonia

Display typefaces

Since they are different in aspect from each other and the fact that there is no general rule that surrounds and defines the Display family, they can express the whole range of emotions. They can go from apathy to depression, from a complete childish involvement and joy to some suited, scary seriousness business feeling (the latter definition is usually expression of some monospaced typefaces).

Like every other typeface, more specifically here, every change in weight and style brings in a new sentiment to the table: use it in bold and your content will be strong, fierce; change it to a lighter italic and it will look like its moving, ready to exit from the page.

As such, they take years to master and we advice not to use them on your first web work, unless you are completely sure of what you are doing.

Every font communicates differently, on a conscious as well as on a subconscious level; even within the same typeface, it all comes down to what we are accustomed to.

In the case of font color, what a script does and feel in the European culture can drastically change if the same is used for advertising in the Asian market.

[Always do your research first.]

Combining typefaces

Combining typefaces is a vital aspect of your projects but it's a tool that is hard to master.

Generally, it is said that you should use no more than two fonts in your design. It is a good rule; but let me explain it — or better — enlarge it.

While working with text for an informational text block, similar to the one you are reading now, stick to it. You will express enough contrast and interest while staying balanced and the reader will not get distracted. They will follow the flow and understand the hierarchy of what they are reading.

However, as a designer, while typesetting you're not always working on a pure text block: you could be working with words on a packaging or on the web.

However, if you know enough about typography and your eyes are well trained (usually after years of visual research and of designing with attention) you can break the rules. You get energy only when mixing contrasting fonts, so why not add a third one to bring in a better balance between the two?

As a rule, you can combine fonts when:

- They are not in the same classification. You mix fonts to add contrast and energy and to inject interest and readability in your document and this is why the clash between serif and sans has been proven timeless. Working with two serifs/sans together instead works only with extensive trial and error and you should choose two fonts that carry enough differences.

- You can usually combine different subfamilies, for example a slab serif with a modern one or a geometric sans with a grotesque.

- If your scope is readability, find the same structure. A similar height and similar width works easily when choosing two classifications; but if your scope is aesthetic for small portions of text, you can try completely different structures, such as a slab serif with a geometric sans. You will see that sometimes it does the job!

- Go extreme! This requires more experience to balance it out, but if you're working with display or script typefaces, it's almost impossible to find something similar without being boring or unreadable. Try to mix them with more simplistic typefaces if the starting point has a lot of decorations; you won't regret the trial!

Typography properties

Now that you know the families, you need to know the general rules that will make your text and their usage flow like a springtime breeze.

Kerning

Is the adjusting of space between two characters to achieve a visually balanced word trough and a visually equal distribution of white space.

The word originates from the Latin word *cardo* meaning hinge. When letters were made of metal on wooden blocks, parts of them were built to hang off the base, thus giving space for the next character to sit closer.

Tracking

Tracking is also as called *letter-spacing* and it is concerned with the entire word—not single characters or the whole text block—to change the density and texture in a text and to affect its readability.

The word originates from the metal tracks where the wooden blocks with the characters were moved horizontally.

Tracking

Tracking request careful settings: too much white space and the words won't appear as single coherent blocks anymore – reduce the white space between the letters drastically and the letters themselves won't be readable.

As a rule, you want your lines of text to be made of 50 to 75 characters, including dots and spaces, to achieve better readability. Some will ask you to stop your typing as soon as approximately 39 characters are reached, but I tend to differ.

Ligatures

According to kerning, especially on serifs, two or three character can clash together. Ligatures are born to avoid this; they are stylistic characters that combine two or three letters into one letter:

- Standard ligatures are naturally and functionally the most common ones and are made between **fi**, **fl**, and other letters when placed next to an f. They should be used, as they tend to make the script more legible.

- Discretionary ligatures are not functional, they just serve a decorative purpose. They are commonly found and designed between **Th** and **st**; as mentioned previously, you should use them at your discretion.

ff fl st ct ffi fi

Leading

Leading is the space between the baselines of your text, while line-height adds to the notions and also to the height of ascenders and descenders. The name came to be because in the ancient times, stripes of lead were used to add white space between two lines of text.

There are many rules in typesetting (none of which came out as a perfect winner) and everything changes according to the typeface you're using.

Mechanical print tends to add 2 points to the current measure being used, while a basic rule for digital is to scale the line-spacing as much as 120 percent of your x-height, which is called *single spacing*.

As a rule of thumb, scale in between 120 and 180 percent and you are good to go (of course with the latter being used for typefaces with a major x-height). Just remember, the descenders should never touch the next line ascenders, otherwise the eye will perceive the text as crumpled and you will have difficulties to understand where one line ends and the other start.

Is the space between the baselines of

Information hierarchy – giving order to your text

This is important in a text because it helps the reader understand the order of the text, what's more important, what's regular text, what requires attention, and also with the use of descriptive titles it helps him skip entire parts of the text that are of no specific interest.

To achieve the aspect of a title and of a sub-title, different sizes and weights are used between the two parts. We generally prefer to triple the dimension of the actual text and go with the corresponding leading directly above it; if a subtitle is present, leading can be adjusted from 100 to 110 percent.

I'M A TITLE

And I'm the most classic
lorem ipsum text!

I bet you know me!

Alignments

This book is written in English, actually aiming at the western cultures, which we tend to read and write from left to right; hence, the alignment of it's type follows the same direction.

It depends on your culture and whom your text is aimed to. It also depends on the general aesthetic that you're trying to achieve and usually compromises between the two needs to be fulfilled.

Scientifically speaking, centrally aligned text is the weakest from a readability point of view: your eye can't find a consistent starting and stopping point. So, every passage will automatically adjust every new line in an instant; it's a subtle but catastrophic step, since the focus will be shifted from the word to the general picture. People tend to be easily distracted when reading a text that is centrally aligned.

So, both left and right edges are good for typesetting; it depends on your language and aesthetics.

It reside on your culture and who your text is aimed to. It also depend on the general aesthetic you're trying to achieve – and usually compro-mises between the two need to be done.	It reside on your culture and who your text is aimed to. It also depend on the general aesthetic you're trying to achieve – and usually compro-mises between the two need to be done.	It reside on your culture and who your text is aimed to. It also depend on the general aesthetic you're trying to achieve – and usually compro-mises between the two need to be done.

Rag

It's a term and a direct consequence of your alignment; it's the uneven vertical edge in a block of type.

A good rag goes in and out from the margin in small increments; while a bad, distracting one creates distracting shapes.

This can be managed by manually adjusting line breaks or by editing the copy:

It deserve a sepa-rate paragraph from the align-ments, since every feature, every defect that can is made visi-ble with an ali-gned text – when the same text is justified tends to be exaggerated. It *Weird shapes*	It deserve a separate paragraph from the ali-gnments, since every feature, every defect that can is made visible with an aligned text – when the same text is justified tends to be exaggerated. It can be full, left, right or cen-tered, with the terms referring to the align- *Better rag*

Justification of text

It deserves a separate paragraph from the alignments, since every feature and every defect can be made visible with an aligned text; when the same text is justified, it tends to be exaggerated. It can be *full*, *left*, *right*, or *centered* with the terms referring to the alignment of the last line of text.

It's a common type of text alignment in print, where the spaces between words are stretched or compressed to align the left and right edges of the text equally.

This commonly gives birth to various issues, as a loose line where the space is just too much, or a tight one, where the text is too crumpled.

The centered one especially gives birth to *rivers*, which are gaps in the text that appear to run almost vertically and are bad for readability, since they distract the eye.

One good test for you to discover rivers in your typesetting is to take the paper or the text and rotate it by 180 degrees, turning it upside down.

Doing so will make the words and text less easy to be recognized by the brain, which will now concentrate more on the actual shape of your paragraph, instead of its meaning, which will allow you to see them better.

A good test for rivers it to turn the text upside down, since the brain will less likely recognize words and will concentrate more on the surroun- ding.	A good test for rivers it to turn the text upside down, since the brain will less likely recognize words and will concentrate more on the surroun- ding.	A good test for rivers it to turn the text upside down, since the brain will less likely recognize words and will concentrate more on the surroun- ding.

Rivers

Summary

The preceding text covers the basics of typography, which you should study and know in order to make the text in your assignment flow better.

Now, you have a greater understanding of typography: what it is; what it's made of; what are its characteristics; what the brain search for and process in a text; the lengths it will go to understand it; and the alignments, spacing, and other issues that revolve around this beautiful subject.

The most important rule to remember is that text is used to express something. It may be an informative reading, may be the expression of a feeling, such as a poem, or it can be something to make you feel something specifically.

Every text has a feeling, every text has an inner tone of voice that can be expressed visually through typography. Usually it's the text itself that dictates its feeling – and help you decide which and how to express it.

All the preceding rules, properties, and knowledge are means for you to express it and there's a large range of properties on the Web for you to use them. There is almost as much variety available in print with properties for leading, kerning, tracking, and typographical hierarchy all built in your browsers,

We'll start to explore them in the upcoming chapters.

2
Responsive Typography

We have learnt all the basics of typography, and now we will learn how to apply them to the Web through simple HTML and CSS.

We'll learn how to stylize the written content on your website by creating the page and going through CSS properties.

In this chapter, we will cover the following topics in detail:

- Creating the page
- Using CSS properties
- Ligatures
- Hierarchy
- Example and exercise to use the typography rules!

Creating the page

Before exploring the wonderful world of online typography, we need to set up the space for it to fully develop; so we are going to create a simple HTML5 page to populate with our written content.

```
<!DOCTYPE html>
<html lang="en">
  <head>
    <meta charset="utf-8">
    <title>Your typography resource</title>
    <link rel="stylesheet" href="../style.css">
  </head>
  <body>
  </body>
</html>
```

See? No complex data, import nothing. Just an empty page.

Since we're going to concentrate on type and type alone, we're not going to add a variety of elements or a complex layout.

Just a couple of simple lines of text will do, they will show you exactly what we are working on and how it's working.

So we're adding a `<p>` tag to the body:

```
<!DOCTYPE html>
<html lang="en">
  <head>
    <meta charset="utf-8">
    <title>Your typography resource</title>
    <link rel="stylesheet" href="../style.css">
  </head>
  <body>
    <p>I am a simple line of text. I am a simple line of text.
       I am a simple line of text. I am a simple line of text.</p>
  </body>
</html>
```

A **P** element in HTML stands for **Paragraph**. It's a basic CSS1 selector, supported by all the browsers; it's used to encapsulate text. As a default property, it is packed with 1em margins that can be specified and modified through CSS. It is a block element, meaning that it won't allow other portions of the page to sit next to it (by default). When the HTML5 standard was introduced, the align property (specifiable by left, right, center, and justify), for the inside alignment of text, was deprecated. The `</>` closing tag can be omitted for elements like `<address>`, `<article>`, `<aside>`, `<blockquote>`, `<div>`, `<dl>`, `<fieldset>`, `<footer>`, `<form>`, `<h1>`, `<h2>`, `<h3>`, `<h4>`, `<h5>`, `<h6>`, `<header>`, `<hr>`, `<menu>`, `<nav>`, `<ol>`, `<pre>`, `<section>`, `<table>`, `<ul>` or another `<p>` element, or if there is no more content in the parent element and the parent element is not an `<a>` element.

The following image shows the standard output for the preceding code on any browser:

I am a simple line of text. I am a simple line of text. I am a simple line of text. I am a simple line of text.

As you can see, it's pretty straightforward; no line break, no spacing, and nothing more than pure text.

Adding another `<p>` after it will add another text line. Please note that the correct way to address the space between them is with the margins CSS property and not by adding `<br>` elements or empty paragraphs between them.

I am a simple line of text. I am a simple line of text. I am a simple line of text. I am a simple line of text.

I am a simple line of text. I am a simple line of text. I am a simple line of text. I am a simple line of text.

Let's wander through CSS

It's time to add some CSS properties to the preceding `<p>`.

They are generally divided into three big groups: font, text and letter, and finally the other ones; where the latter are single properties without a prefix.

Font is a group dictating the general characteristics. It is the overall style and weight of the text and letter; it deals with single characters, spaces, words, and so on.

Also, as a difference between the two groups, the font declaration can be minimized in one single big declaration, while text and letter all are single specific calls to determined properties.

So lets take a look at them in our CSS.

Font-family is used to define the typeface you want for your content. It can either contain one or more specifically aimed typefaces, with the exact family names enclosed between " " (double quotes), generic family names instead can be written without quotes; its application depends on each computer, on its installed typefaces and on the browser support of that particular request. Your first choice will have to be written first, followed by the substitutive families in case the loading or finding on the guest computer of the specifical font fails; 'if it fail, the browser will then move to the next declared family until the very last one, which being generic will tell the browser to load a web-safe font of that family.

Relying on the web-safe fonts is a good thought, but as of today that limitation is disappearing. We'll learn more about this in the next chapter. The following code is an example of the font-family:

```
p { font-family: "Georgia", "Times New Roman", Times, serif; }
```

In this case, we made the change from a standard sans to a more classic serif, Georgia, with some generic backup. As in the preceding section, the browser will first search for the font named Georgia on the computer; if it doesn't find it, it will search for Times New Roman and then for the Times family; and last, if all else fails, it will apply a generic serif.

In fact, finding Times New Roman on our computer will display the sample text as the following image:

> I am a simple line of text.I am a simple line of text.I am a simple line of text.

Font-style is generally used to define italic portions of text – since its variables are limited to: normal, italic and oblique - whereas oblique is a slanted version of the normal weight and style, also called faux-italic.

 Faux-italic (in this web case oblique) is an angled version of the regular, normal typeface. It can look and may also feel correct from time to time, depending on specific typefaces. But it is surely better to use the true italic version of the typeface you're using when available.

Italics generally differ from the regular style, as they serve a different purpose and visual and the type designer have addressed that matter in the best way possible; sometimes by modifying or copying faux-italics shapes as well, if the aim of the font is to reminiscence a certain era when they were present. Even in that case, the italic typeface that has been designed, render, print, and feel better (last one thankful to optical corrections) than its slanted brother.

Unfortunately, people today are so used to faux-italics and bolds that they don't even notice anymore, all thanks to Microsoft Office that prior to recent versions enlisted just one regular font from an installed typeface and when clicked (as well as bold) just slanted it. The following code is an example of font-style:

```
p { font-style: italic; }
```

It will render as follows:

> *I'm a simple line of text.I'm a simple line of text. I'm a simple line of text. I'm a simple line of text.*

Ironically, the default text it took without any other declaration has no italic, so it reverted to faux one.

Font-size is easy to understand; it sets the size of the font. It can be expressed in pixels, em, and percentages, differences between them will be looked at later.

The declaration is straightforward and there is no need to explain it.

```
p { font-size: 24px; }
```

I'm a simple line of text.I'm a simple line of text.

If it's not defined, the browser will give it the default value, usually 16px. Also other values are available, like xx-large, x-large, larger, large, medium, small, smaller, x-small, xx-small, and so on. You get them by the name, each of them referring to the very first defined, or not-defined, value. But you'll probably never use them, as simple as they are.

Font-variant is straightforward tool and it defines the usage or not of small-caps. It can be declared as the latest or as normal.

```
p { font-variant: small-caps; }
```

I'M A SIMPLE LINE OF TEXT.I'M A SIMPLE LINE OF TEXT. I'M A SIMPLE LINE OF TEXT. I'M A SIMPLE LINE OF TEXT.

Font-weight allows you to choose the weight of the font, with values as light, lighter, and normal, 100, 200, 300, 400, 500, 600, 700, 800, 900, bold, and bolder.

Numbers of course refer to specified weights of your chosen typeface, but you'll generally end up using bold or light, never lighter or bolder.

```
p { font-weight: bold; }
```

I'm a simple line of text.I'm a simple line of text. I'm a simple line of text. I'm a simple line of text.

Font-stretch is a newborn CSS3 property that defines the stretching of the font on your website. It can be declared as normal, condensed, and expanded (condensed and expanded with the addition of ultra, extra, and semi for different levels of amusement).

```
p { font-stretch: semi-expanded; }
```

I'm a simple line of text. I'm a simple line of text. I'm a simple line of text.

Sadly it seems like neither the last version of Firefox nor Chrome supports this property, as it can be seen in the preceding image. But believe me, it exist!

As mentioned at the start of the chapter, all of the preceding properties can be combined into a single-giant declaration, usually called shorthand and still respect the CSS standards.

The following are the rules:

- Font-size and family must be declared, otherwise the overall will be ignored

- Font-family must be declared last

- Every other font property can be declared without order, as long as it come before font-size

- Remember to add spaces between each property, to enclose the exact name families between double quotes, and to divide a generic one with a comma

Let's take a look at:

```
p { font: bold small-caps italic expanded 24px Times, serif;
    font: bold small-caps italic 24px Times, serif; }
```

I'M A SIMPLE LINE OF TEXT

The second, almost-the-same, declaration is really important. As **font-stretch** is a recent and unsupported property, it can get the browser to ignore your whole declaration and not render the P as you want to.

Making a CSS3 fallback shorthand is a must, if the first gets ignored as a whole then the second won't and your font will be rendered correctly as requested.

Up to letter and text group!

Now that we explained the font subgroup, we can jump to the letter, text, and more. As a quick rule, remember that these are more specific, aimed at single characters than font.

Color will allow you to choose the text color, with values as:

- Names, for web-safe colors, such as yellow, red, black, green, cyan, and white.

- Hexadecimal values (`#ff0000`, `#000000` – or `#000` since couple of same characters can be combined into one, saving bits in your CSS file).

- RGB and RGBA values are simple numeric values. The A in RGBA stands for transparency, it varies from 0 (transparent) to 1 (completely opaque).The following code shows exactly that: the first line color is expressed trough name, then hexadecimal and hexadecimal compressed formula; after that RGB and RGBA values.

```
p { color: red;
    color: #ff0000;
    color: #f00;
    color: 255, 0, 0;
    color: 255, 0, 0, 1;}
```

All the preceding parts of code are various ways to write and obtain the same result, such as this:

```
I'm a simple line of text.I'm a simple line of text. I'm a simple line of text. I'm a simple line of text.
```

Letter-spacing is usually seen as the application of Kerning on the Web. While its not a completely correct definition (as it doesn't really work on single letter kerning, it touches spacing in the whole word). It defines the space between each letter in the words and as such, it kind of works. Values run from normal, number 0 to prevent justifying and numerical/percentage values. It can also be used with negative ones.

```
p { letter-spacing: 5px; }
```

CSS3 added a rule, which is currently not well supported and is a little bit different from letter-spacing: **Font-kerning**.

```
I'm  a  simple  line  of  text.I'm  a  simple  line  of  text.
```

Font-kerning allows the adjustments of inter-glyph spacing, as written inside the current font, it won't allow for the letter-to-letter adjust, it's a mere specification between the usage and the choice to not use kerning as provided by the used font.

An image is better than thousand words, so let's take a look at the following image:

```
I am using the provided font kerning instructions. AW VA

I am not using the provided font kerning instructions. AW VA
```

The first example is:

```
p { font-kerning: normal; }
```

The second is:

```
p { font-kerning: none; }
```

This rule allows for no values other than the on/off ones (and an auto, discretionary one that leave the choice to the browser), but the difference is clearly visible in the last couple of letters in the preceding image. As the second p is not using the inside written kerning rules, AW and VA start to spread around.

 Also, its worth noticing that we're still referring to the metrical kerning, no solution have been made for optical corrections.

Text-align is born after the deprecation of the align element. Its values are the same: left, right, center, and justify.

```
p { text-align: center; }
```

This is how it looks:

I'm a simple line of text.I'm a simple line of text.

Text-decoration serves to focus or define some appearances in the informational text. Values are: none, underline, overline, line through, and blink

For the sake of brevity, I'm going to write multiple p's and id each one of them to show you the different decorations in one single image. Blink requires a screen to be seen, it cannot be made visible on the printed page since it will be an animation: in one instant text will be visible, in the next it won't. It was used in the ancient times of the Web to display links.

It is also now deprecated and it doesn't work anymore.

```
p { text-decoration: underline; }
```

The following image shows the output of the underline command:

I'm a simple line of text.I'm a simple line of text.

The following image shows the output of the `overline` command:

```
p { text-decoration: overline; }
```

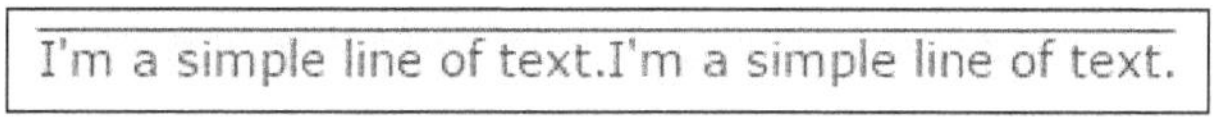

I'm a simple line of text.I'm a simple line of text.

The following image shows the output of the `line through` command:

```
p { text-decoration: line through; }
```

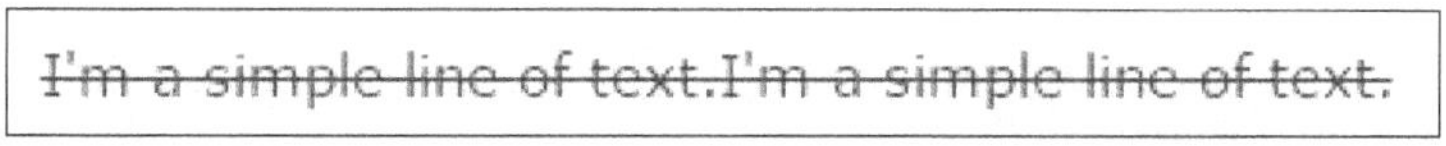

~~I'm a simple line of text.I'm a simple line of text.~~

Text-indent serves to move inward the very first line of text of a paragraph. The value can be based on pixels (absolute) or percentages and it can't be a negative value, or else it will be ignored.

```
p { text-indent: 20px; }
```

This is how an indented line looks:

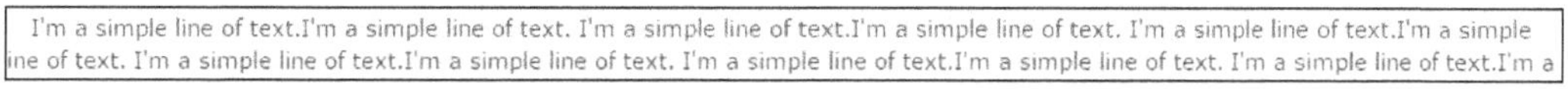

I'm a simple line of text.I'm a simple line of text. I'm a simple line of text.I'm a simple line of text. I'm a simple line of text.I'm a simple line of text. I'm a simple line of text.I'm a simple line of text. I'm a simple line of text.I'm a simple line of text. I'm a simple line of text.I'm a

Text-transform serves to control the appearance of the letters in a determined text. You can choose between none, capitalize, lowercase, and uppercase. Each value is self-explanatory.

```
p { text-transform: capitalize; }
```

This is how it looks after capitalization:

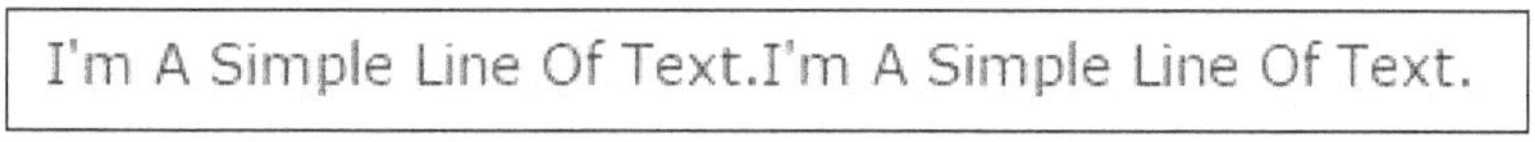

I'm A Simple Line Of Text.I'm A Simple Line Of Text.

In the modern times, the property **Font-variant-caps** have been introduced with CSS3 but it is still missing a wide, safe support to use it.

The numerous values are built inside, like normal, small-caps, all-small-caps, petite-caps, all-petite-caps, unicase, and titling-caps.

- **Small-caps** explains itself
- **All-small-caps** will apply small-caps to the first letters and the capitalized ones, giving it a better and coherent appearance
- **Petite-caps** allow the visualization of petite capitals
- **Unicase** allows the mixture of uppercase characters (when typed as) and lowercase ones
- **Titling-caps** are a variety of all-caps, since they are designed to be less strong than the text set in all capitals

The following is the code which explains font-variant-caps with its values:

```
p { font-variant-caps: all-petite-caps; }
```

This is how it looks:

I'M A SIMPLE LINE OF TEXT.

Text-shadow is a CSS3 property to stylize your content. As the name says, it simply adds a shadow to the text. The values can be either positive or negative and they can be mixed; they must be expressed in numerical absolute characters, followed by the color name or hexadecimal or rgb/rgba definition. The first value is horizontal, second is vertical, and an optional third for Blur can be specified as well.

Also, the multiple shadows can be combined by just writing them on, or after, the other in the same declaration will do the trick and all will be applied.

```
p { text-shadow: 2px 2px 8px #FF0000; }
```

This is how it will look:

I'm a simple line of text.

Use this property subtly for best results, don't abuse it.

Text-overflow is the CSS3 property that allows you to give an indication that more content is underlying, but that is breaking its inline boundaries given by the container a little bit like the **Read more…** segment that is visible in WordPress posts.

The Text-overflow values are the following ones:

- **Clip** is the default. It truncates the word whenever an overflow occurs, even in the middle of a character.
- **Ellipsis** shows a "…" for the clipped text. It will take space inside the content, thus displaying even less text than before. Also, if enough space is not available for it to be visible, the ellipsis will be truncated too!
- **Visible**: The over flown text will be left visible, expanding outside the content area
- (""): Text enclosed in double quotes or empty string between double quotes will behave as clip, but it will truncate in-between two characters, single characters will be left untouched and won't be cropped.
- **String** inserts any value between single quotes and will show it as the truncated text signal.

The following is the code which explains text-overflow with its values:

```
p { text-overflow: clip; }
```

This is how it looks:

> I'm a simple line of text. I'm a simple line of text. I'm a simple

Direction serves to control the appearance of your writing in the browser. Ltr is the default value, meaning left-to-right text; Rtl does the opposite, rendering your text from right to left. The following code shows how direction works:

```
p { direction: rtl; }
```

This is how it looks:

> .I'm a simple line of text.I'm a simple line of text. I'm a simple line of text. I'm a simple line of text

This doesn't seem like much is changing, but the dots are now placed before the text (at least in our appearance, seems we read from left to right) and text will be automatically aligned on the right edge.

White-space is explained by the name itself and it's tracking plus blank space addition in Web Design. The values are strange and need a bit of explanation:

- **normal**: The sequence of white spaces will collapse and the text will wrap to the next line when needed

- **nowrap**: The sequences will collapse but the text will never wrap to the following line, practically staying on one single line and breaking your elements

- **pre** will take all the white space and the line breaks and force the browser to show them, not allowing for any wrapping. This is useful if you're displaying a code.

- **pre-line** and **pre-wrap** practically act as normal, with words wrapping when necessary and on defined line breaks

Detailed steps to download the code bundle are mentioned in the Preface of this book. Please have a look.

The code bundle for the book is also hosted on GitHub at `https://github.com/PacktPublishing/Practical-Responsive-Typography`. We also have other code bundles from our rich catalog of books and videos available at `https://github.com/PacktPublishing/`. Check them out!

The following code shows how white-space is implemented:

```
p { white-space: nowrap; }
```

This is how it looks:

I'm a simple line of text. I'm a simple line of text. I'm a simple line

As you can see, words won't wrap and will exit your div with a set width. Pre-wrap will practically add a lot of white space before the line. You better leave this property as default, not specifying it in 99% of the cases.

Word-wrap is similar to the preceding case but it's a CSS3 only introduced rules and it's way better than white-space. It also addresses a different properly (but in your end result sometime it will appear that the result is the same). It does not address the surrounding white spaces and is aimed at the longer words, thus allowing them to break into syllables when the browser feels that they're going to break the container element width (as seen in the preceding example)

The values are really interesting and useful (when the browser supports it of course)

- **normal**: This only breaks words when standard
- **break-word**: Even if it isn't grammatically correct, this property value will allow unbreakable words to be broken.

```
I'm a simple line of text.
I'm a simple line of text.
I'masimplelineoftextI'ma
simplelineoftext.
```

As you can see, the long and unbreakable word with no white-space has been broken completely, respecting your container width. Useful, isn't it?

Word-spacing only addresses the white space between couples of words, leaving tracking and kerning untouched. Negative values are allowed, normal is default or specific pixels or percentages value.

```
p { word-spacing: 50px; }
```

This is how it looks:

```
I'm    a    simple    line    of    text.
```

Line-height is an extremely important rule for your design, as explained in the first chapter of this book. Normal value, the default one, will apply the line-height that is defined in the font file.

You can define it as single, double, or multiple using the fixed 1, 2, n numeric values; you can define it with a fixed, pixel value as 10px, 20px, and so on or the best way to use it, especially for our future look into a responsive Web design is to use percentages.

On the Web, the default print rule of 120% seems a little too cluttered, while perfectly readable. I usually suggest implementing it from 130%/150% on, especially for a small amount of text.

```
p { line-height: 150%; }
```

This is how it looks:

> I'm a simple line of text. I'm a simple line of text.I'm a simple line of text.
>
> I'm a simple line of text. I'm a simple line of text.I'm a simple line of text.
>
> I'm a simple line of text. I'm a simple line of text. I'm a simple line of text.
>
> I'm a simple line of text. I'm a simple line of text. I'm a simple line of text.

Transform is a CSS3 property that is not specifically made for the text part of a website but is clearly applicable and useful in that case as well, so it's better for us to study it.

It allows for 2D and 3D transformation of a given element, such as rotations, scale, skew, movement, and so on.

Default value is none, otherwise you'll need to transform them with the addition of one of these suffixes:

- scale: (x value, y value) as fixed ones or percentages
- scale3d (simply add the z value) x, y, z values can also be used separately
- rotate (angle); angle expressed for example, as 10deg
- rotate3d (x, y, z values)
- skew (x-angle, y-angle); if you want to express them separately you need to write: skewX and skewY as two separate properties
- translate (x, y) or translate3d (x, y, z) or translateX translate as separate properties

Note that the preceding section, while we're referring to text, indicates pure movement and not a language translation.

```
p { transform:rotate(45deg); }
```

This is how it looks:

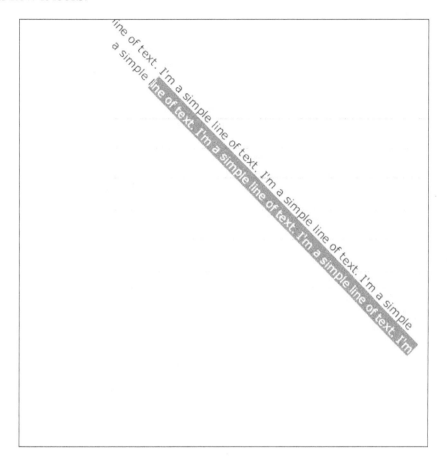

As you can see in preceding the image, the text is rendered by the browser and it is selectable and readable by SEO bots without any problem. With prior decisions and design aid out, this allows for some graphical page without the use of images. You'll just have to experiment with it. Keep in mind that the mobile browser support may be low at the time of writing.

You can learn more on CSS transform on the w3school dedicated page:

```
http://www.w3schools.com/cssref/css3_pr_transform.asp
```

Or on the Mozilla developers' page:

```
https://developer.mozilla.org/en-US/docs/Web/CSS/CSS_Transforms/
Using_CSS_transforms
```

Vertical-align is the other property that is not only for text but can be extremely useful for typesetting. As the name indicates, it defines the alignment of an object on a vertical base based on the appearance and characteristic of its container. So it's directly applicable to the p and not to the container itself.

The values are easy and are top, bottom, middle, and baseline (they explain themselves pretty well) with two additions:

- **text-top** will place the element it applied to at the top of the font of the parent element
- **text-bottom** will align the object, its applied to, to the bottom of the font of the parent element

Also for text, there is the super value that will make the text behave similar to a superscript:

```
.s { vertical-align: super; }
```

This is how it looks:

I am a simple line of ^{text}.

Of course it does its best with numbers, but you get the idea

Recently with CSS3, the **font-variant-position** property has been made, which allows for natural, stylistic super, and subscript

Values are normal, sub, and super:

```
.s { font-variant-position: sub; }
```

This is how it looks:

I'm a simple li$_2$ne of text.

 At the moment of writing, it seems like the latest version of Google Chrome and doesn't support this property but Firefox 38.0 does. So use it with caution.

When the time will be right, the numeric control will be a breeze over the Web, giving even a better look to your pages, thankful to **font-variant-numeric** property.

- Normal is the standard, unapplied value
- Lining-nums enables the use of lining forms
- Oldstyle-nums shows the numbers in old style
- Proportional-nums show proportional number values
- Tabular-nums is called when a table alignment is needed
- Diagonal-fractions shows the fractions properly, not as numbers with a slash in between
- Stacked fractions allow the display of lining stacked fractions
- Ordinal acts as the name says
- Slashed-zero uses the alternate zero where available

All of the preceding is possible as a beautiful mixture of property, just remember that each one will slow down the page loading time and that you need to leave a blank space between each couple.

```
p { font-variant-numeric: lining-nums slashed-zero }
```

This is how it looks next to a font that doesn't support it:

> I'm a simple line of text with some 0123456 in it
>
> I'm a simple line of text with some 0123456 in it

font-variant-alternates is a way to achieve alternate glyphs and decorative swashes and it's a kind of long, complicated property, since it aims for specific characters inside the fonts.

@font-feature-values is font specific, it will be followed by the exact name of the font – for example, @font-feature-values Times New Roman {}

Or if declared later as a standard, CSS element rule will be written like this:

```
p { font-family: Bookmania;
    font-variant-alternates:  swash (chosen); }
```

Other property's values are:

- Historical-forms is a simple activation of display features
- Stylistic, styleset, character-variant, swash, ornaments, annotation requires more work, since they need specific values

```
@font-feature-values Bookmania {
    @swash { flower: 1; chosen: 2; }
}
```

The preceding call for example searches and displays the first and second alternate swashes inside the Bookmania font and will display it as shown:

I'm A 𝒜 simple line of text with a swash on the B 𝓑

The flower and the preceding name is chosen by you, who writes the code for each font, to be able to address it specifically later.

```
The rule, written like the following exampleH1:first-letter { font-
variant-alternates: swash(chosen); }
```

It will define that the first Heading will place the desired swash (the second in the whole font) as the first letter for stylistic purposes.

Other rules are available but won't be useful, so we're not going to take a look at them.

Instead, let's explore ligatures.

Ligatures

Ligatures are important as they guarantee a better flow of legibility of the text and better readability of a word when some characters clash.

In fact, they are usually added, or better designed, when two letters are joined as a single one. This usually happens when two letters have ascenders, like ff, ft, that clash together producing a rather unpleasant result.

Even the ampersand symbol is born as a ligature, when the et in the handwritten Latin text where combined.

So, how we can apply them to the Web?

CSS3 standard introduces the property **font-variant-ligatures** to precisely address the matter through numerous values, such as:

- Common-ligatures - no-common-ligatures
- Discretionary-ligatures - no-discretionary-ligatures
- Historical-ligatures - no-historical-ligatures
- Contextual - no-contextual
- Normal and none.

Each property can be declared with multiple values, containing all of the preceding declared values..

For example, if you like discretionary but not historical ligatures, you can write your property as follows

```
p { font-variant-ligatures: discretionary-ligatures no-historical-
ligatures; }
```

Unfortunately, similar to all CSS3, it is still widely unsupported, so use it carefully.

If you want ligatures in your web text and I don't see why you would not want them you can use this old property, which is not of any CSS standard but it's supported on the majority of new and old browsers:

Text-rendering is a simple, non-customizable function that tells the rendering engine how to optimize text. It can be set to:

- optimizeSpeed value rendering speed at the most, disabling kerning and tracking. If your site is high on text and you don't want to slow down page load, and then this one is for you.
- optimizeLegibility is more interesting for designers. It reduces page speed loading time but allows the usage of kerning and ligatures (with no options to set unfortunately).
- geometricPrecision lets you scale your text fluidly in responsive design, with the most sharp appearances. Its widely supported by WebKit engines and is treated like optimizeLegibility by Gecko's ones.

The following code shows how text-rendering is implemented:

```
p { text-rendering: optimizeLegibility: }
```

This is how it looks:

I'm a simple line of text with a fi ligature .

Image shows my favorite friendly serif of all time, Bookmania by Mark Simonson, one of the best typographers of all time, as originally rendered by Mozilla Firefox 38.0.1

The Web is limited when you talk about ligatures and you can't do more than the preceding two things unless you want to go back to the nineties and use an image for your title or text and I seriously advice against that in 2016.

Hierarchy

Another important thing to learn, which will require that the preceding rules are applied, is hierarchy.

Its been explained in the previous chapter, it's application in the Web world is pretty straightforward.

Don't do it wrong, don't just use p with different ids. There are HTML elements since the first versions that will be rendered are better, they will be correctly read from SEO robots: the Headings elements.

They are numbered and ordered from the first to the sixth, from H1 to H6, they render correctly and differently, by default, on any browser but they are modifiable through all the preceding rules.

So you can modify their appearance any way you want, just remember to address that part correctly, with h1 being the most prominent and h6 the least. As much as they are important for your website SEO, in this book we're covering more than the writing and the visual aspect of the matter; so as a general rule, remember that every text is readable at a glance if it incorporates three levels: Primary, Secondary, and Tertiary.

Primary is an h1 or h2 (if the h1 is already present somewhere on the page, remember that you can correctly use more than one h1 in the same page, if each one is in a different section of the page, but this will still create some confusion for the SEO). The secondary level must be the following heading in this order and Tertiary is your principal informative text.

All said and done, remember that the above CSS rules and properties apply to every part of the text you want, be it a link, a title, or a focus point.

Example and exercise!

Now for a little fun (only studying without practicing is something that makes anyone mad, as a sometime teacher and all-time student I know that very well – hey, don't judge me wrong, you really never stop to learn!), it's time to see if those rules are used in the real world, ready or not, here we go!

Let's go through the practice exercise:

- Let's find a text that we like so that it will be easier for everyone involved if we know it, to divide it into the required three level faster.

- The text that we'll choose is going to be different from each reader, so whatever level you see or want to apply is ok. We're going to need them to visually differentiate things.

- I hereby choose one of my favourite poems of all time – or better, part of it, since it's really long: *Nothing but Death* by *Pablo Neruda*

    Pablo Neruda, Nothing but Death – 1926

    There are cemeteries that are lonely,

    graves full of bones that do not make a sound,

    the heart moving through a tunnel,

    in it darkness, darkness, darkness,

    like a shipwreck we die going into ourselves,

    as though we were drowning inside our hearts,

    as though we lived falling out of the skin into the soul.

- This is our informative text. For a Primary Level I'll be using the Title – and for Secondary Author name and publishing data.

- So, let's see how it looks in the browser, shall we?

> Pablo Neruda, Nothing but Death – 1926 There are cemeteries that are lonely, graves full of bones that do not make a sound, the heart moving through a tunnel, in it darkness, darkness, darkness, like a shipwreck we die going into ourselves, as though we were drowning inside our hearts, as though we lived falling out of the skin into the soul.

As a single <p>, despite the feeling, the soul of the poem itself – well, everything get lost. You wouldn't really care about reading it, would you?

Luckily, HTML and CSS are here to help us: first, we're going to divide the text into three levels as shown:

```
<h1>Nothing but Death</h1>
<h2>Pablo Neruda - 1926</h2>
<p> There are cemeteries that are lonely[…]</p>
```

Remember, as the last element in our page, we're not obligated to use the close tag on our paragraph, its just better to do so as a standard.

Nothing but Death

Pablo Neruda - 1926

There are cemeteries that are lonely[...]

Way better already!

Hierarchy has been established, information layout is better, but don't forget to add a `<br>` element at the end of each line since it's a poem and its verses lengths has been given.

It's time to polish everything with CSS and with what we learnt in this chapter. We won't be doing graphically heavy retouches, such as pure CSS driven 3D text or Inset one and so on, it's not the scope of this book; we're going to work on a better flow for the eye

```
* {   text-rendering: optimizeLegibility;
      font-weight: normal;
      margin: 10px 15px;
}

h1 { font-family: "Georgia", "Times New Roman", Times, serif;
      font-size: 48px;
}
h2 { font-family: "Lucida Grande", "Tahoma", sans-serif;
      font-size: 10px;
      font-variant: normal;
      text-transform: uppercase;
      color: #666;
      margin-top: 10px;
      margin-bottom: 20px;
      letter-spacing: 5px;
```

```
    }
p { font-family: "Georgia", "Times New Roman", Times, serif;
    font-size: 16px;
    line-height: 170%;
    }
```

Note that I've added the top-left margin to the omni selector only for screenshot purposes.

Did you see the following image? Pure CSS at work. How beautiful!

Nothing but Death

PABLO NERUDA · 1926

There are cemeteries that are lonely,

graves full of bones that do not make a sound

the heart moving through a tunnel

in it darkness, darkness, darkness

like a shipwreck we die going into ourselves

as though we were drowning inside our hearts

as though we lived falling out of the skin into the soul

[...]

We'll investigate the given measures later in the book, right now I just tried to achieve a sense of contrasting balance between the H1 and H2, while still preserving legibility; as it's almost a universal solution, thus it can be done with kerning, x-height differences and weight/style, even if in this case I opted for color.

But any of the suggested solution is also good-to-go, it really only depends on what you want to achieve and on the style of the text.

Line-height has been taken into account after the old fashioned "try and try again" method as it varies taking into account line length, font, and reading distance. Please remember that it would need to be changed, when displaying the complete poem, since it would be too loose for the longer text for a short paragraph of it, it actually helps legibility.

Rag unfortunately is not at its best due to the poem structure and with such huge discrepancies, very little to nothing can be done to it.

Ok, so going through this chapter we learned how to stylize your web text and we take a proper shot at it (don't forget to experiment with its values until you are happy, after all the above is just a personal solution).

The intrinsic nature of type

You want to know what's even better about all that we worked on today?

[ Paragraph element is **Naturally Responsive**.]

Yes, you read that right.

The P, seen as a simple container of words is born responsive. Try it, copy-paste one longer chunk of text from this chapter (if you're on a screen of course) inside our exercise <p> and start messing with browser's window width.

The words flow will adjust on itself, following all grammatical rules for hyphenation, word-break, and more.

Of course it won't work this way, so easily for all your websites, especially when contained in another element with a given fixed width.

But still, it's a powerful tool to know.

Summary

Within this chapter you've learnt to apply the properties that we've seen in the first chapter. Properties, such as lineheight, text-shadow, tracking, and kerning are now arrows in your arsenal.

It may take a little while to learn them all but its worth your time, you'll have fun experimenting with them and your projects will be as beautiful and readable as never before! Also, this time, we worked with web-safe fonts.

After all, it was time to study and concentrate a little more on the basic code that on the visual aspect of your text; but in the coming chapter, I'll tell you everything you need to know about more personal, visual font choices!

3
Web Fonts and Services

We've worked 'til now with web safe fonts, which are a very small selection of a beautiful, varied world.

So it's time for us to dive deeper into it, choose from a higher variety of fonts, and make your perfect, custom design readable in our browser without resorting to images – which wouldn't be easily indexable by SEO bots.

We will look at the above using free and paid options, the more the merrier! So we're going to explore them, with their pros and cons.

We are going to guide you through the pros and cons of the most famous services and foundries to embed beautiful typefaces in your websites, using CSS and simple JavaScript so that you'll know which ones are better for you. We will also look at your aims and scope of the project – and why.

After all, aren't you a little bit tired of always using Helvetica or Arial? Have you ever wanted to use Verlag in a safe way on your web pages?

Wonder no more.

The free services for font embedding

Let's take a look at the ones with no price tag, starting with the broader, more interesting choices for us, and for the scope of this book.

CSS @font-face

Even though the `@font-face` rule was born with the CSS2 spec in 1998, it took almost ten years for browser makers to start supporting it – with real, widespread support coming not until a couple of years later.

That is why people usually see it as part of CSS3.

This solution requires you to personally own the license of the fonts you want to use – and to upload them to your server. Being based on self-hosting, it can add to your space and bandwidth fee quite quickly.

But there's an easy solution to that: subsetting.

Subsetting is the practical aspect in owning the fonts: you can take the original font file (usually a .ttf or .otf) and slim it down to only the characters that you need, deleting the unused ones.

This can be done with font editing software, such as the free FontForge or the ultra-famous FontLab. On complex, more complete character map fonts this process brought them down to 50 kb, starting from 600 kb (with only the basic Latin map remaining, which is cool for mono-language, western-focused websites) – resolving the space and bandwidth issues.

This approach, while a cool and fast solution, can easily break your font license.

Since there are a multitude of them, both standard and custom ones from each studio and foundry, you may want to read them to be sure that the font you're using allows modification – and web usage, especially if only the desktop version exists.

Doing so can save you and your company from many lawsuits.

Generally, if you're working on desktop fonts you're not allowed to use them on the web (read your licenses carefully, some of them don't even allow editing of the font files); also, desktop fonts are optimized for print, so they won't render perfectly on the monitor. The best approach would be to purchase the web font directly – some of them even come bundled with the desktop one.

OK, you purchased the correct typeface, you subsetted it: all of the above is useful, but now what?

Now you need to write the code for your font to be addressed correctly by the browser.

The CSS declaration looks like this:

```
@font-face {
  font-family: "Font Family";
  src: url("font.eot");
  src: local(":)"),
    url("font.woff") format("woff"),
    url("font.otf") format("opentype"),
    url("font.svg#filename") format("svg");
```

```
font-weight: normal;
font-style: normal;
}
```

Font family this time will address only our custom specified font – it's an open declaration, meaning you can define it as you want: exact name, all-caps, everything is permitted – even renaming Helvetica to Arial and vice versa.

How evil is that?

Not to worry, just keep it consistent and it will be OK.

What really stand out are the different formats. We named (and are used to) only the .otf here – so what are the others?

The **Web Open Font Format (WOFF)** is a want-to-be worldwide standard format for the fonts on the web, even praised and pushed by the W3C; it contains the TrueType font plus other metadata in a package that is generally compressed by a mighty 40 percent respectful of the original file. It's supported by all major browsers but at different levels, so it still has a long road till it becomes standard.

Despite that, WOFF2 is already out: it features a better, lighter compression than its older brother.

SVG stands for **Scalable Vector Graphics** – it's the standard for readable vectors on the web, since every shape is defined by XML values.

It will just contain and treat every character of the font as a vector, described by various coordinates and values; it weighs less than the original font file – and it can contain multiple fonts in one file! Unfortunately, support is still inconsistent, especially (as always) on Internet Explorer. Way to go, Microsoft!

Also, SVG still doesn't support letter-spacing and hinting – hey, what's that? Don't worry, we'll explain it in later chapters.

Despite that, it's still the most supported custom font solution in mobile browsers on iPhone and iPad, for example. So it's inclusion is mandatory.

EOT (short for **Embedded OpenType**), is a Microsoft proprietary format – yes, you read that right – which is in use only by Internet Explorer. Made in the late nineties, it is a compressed OpenType which also embeds a domain-locking functionality, (it's optional to turn it on), meaning that the specific font can be used only on that domain, preventing it from being stolen.

It was pushed to enter the W3C declarations as a standard web font – and it was twice refused, lastly in favor of the .woff format.

Despite that, Microsoft still use and require it for its browsers – obligating every Web Designer to incorporate it in their works.

 In fact, Internet Explorer won't only use the .eot font: it will ignore every other format, despite their wide support, even crashing on them!

When it comes to its implementation and declaration within the font-face rule – and to avoid the IE bug above, which will make the browser go back to web-safe fonts, we must name the EOT format first, declaring it in a separate source property from the others. Things will go pretty simple this way.

IE will read your declaration and request for specific fonts. If it encounters a format it doesn't recognize and use – it will download it anyway (adding HTTP requests and bandwidth usage), then won't understand it, causing it to completely ignore the @ font-face rule – and ruining your crafted design through the use of web safe fonts.

Way to go, Microsoft: Part II.

Another problem with the standard rule and IE is the fact that this specific browser will jump to the last source property available – writing its declaration separately will allow us to stop exactly at its own font, saving time, bandwidth, and problems.

From there, it is all pretty standard, with a format declaration and a URL for each font file: every other browser will ignore what doesn't belong to it and search for its own compatible format.

The local property

A small thing to pay attention to is the local term: it tells the browser firstly, before anything else (not on IE though), to search and load that font from the visitor computer, saving time with the online download – if the name is specified.

Some time ago, this was a recommended solution to save time – but it came with some problems, like the liberty in naming the font for online, internal use – and more importantly, the fact that more typefaces actually share the same name.

This would have meant that, sometimes, a local computer could have loaded something unwanted, like a different resource that has the same name, ruining and breaking your carefully thought-out layout.

Also worth mentioning is the fact that iOS would have shown a pop-up window to the user, if someone or something was trying to access his local fonts folder (even in this innocent way)

To avoid all these problems, a genius named Paul Irish came in with the smiley idea – since it is a two-byte Unicode character, it is not likely to be the name of a font on a Mac.

Lastly, setting font-weight and font-style to normal in the standard, regular font will allow us to use faux bold and italic on other parts of the site.

 Didn't I say it's a bad thing, earlier in the book? Yes, I did and I won't eat my words. Faux italics and bolds are bad from a typographic point of view.

But if you really need those weights – in a font that doesn't have them designed – it's better for you to have the possibility anyway.

Bold and italic

Even being two different styles of the same typeface, since they are incorporated into different fonts from the regular, we must declare them as different typefaces.

If your font has those styles defined, then you can remove the font-weight and font-style properties from the first declaration, since you won't need them.

You could easily use them for those styles, logically.

The first declaration, aimed at the italic weight would look like this:

```
@font-face {
  font-family: "Font Family";
  font-style: italic;
  font-weight: normal;
  src: url("fontItalic.eot");
  src: local(":)"),
    url("fontItalic.woff") format("woff"),
    url("fontItalic.otf") format("opentype"),
    url("fontItalic.svg#filename") format("svg");
}
```

Here, the same declared typeface name is used with different weights built within. This would mean that using standard em objects within your site will make the CSS automatically call the italic version of your Typeface, even when using and declaring one single name.

Everything is simple, logical, and beautiful.

Unfortunately, for a long time Internet Explorer didn't understand this specific, style-linking declaration, rendering always only the regular font. (Opera also used to have one bug related to this in 10 specific versions, but it's long gone.)

For this reason, a different declaration needed to be made. Way to go, Microsoft: Part III.

And allow me to make a little note now: if you're reading and weren't coding for the web in between the nineties and early '00s, you haven't seen so much of the stuff we were obligated to do for our work so that it performed well on Internet Explorer. Sometimes, completely separate, different code was a must. Some of those horror stories are still told by web programmers today, who gather around a bonfire with a keyboard and a copy of Windows 95 – and you wouldn't believe them.

But they are true, oh they are! And some of those horrible things still crawl and linger somewhere in the web today, behind our beloved screens, in between our clean, functional code. Stay alert, navigator.

OK, break over; time to get back to work! This is the declaration that was meant to work:

```
@font-face {
  font-family: "Italic Font Family";
  src: url("fontItalic.eot");
  src: local(":)"),
    url("fontItalic.woff") format("woff"),
    url("fontItalic.otf") format("opentype"),
    url("fontItalic.svg#filename") format("svg");
}
```

The application of all the above is pretty straightforward. Let's assume you want your website to be written in the fictional "Cool font".

There is nothing simpler than writing your CSS this way:

```
html { font-family: "Cool Font", Georgia, serif; }

@font-face {
  font-family: "Cool Font";
  src: url("font.eot");
  src: local(":)"),
    url("font.woff") format("woff"),
    url("font.otf") format("opentype"),
    url("font.svg#filename") format("svg");
  font-wight: normal;
  font-style: normal;
}
```

A different font with a different declaration for your headings – and you are good to go!

Problems with @font-face

All the previous declarations are correct and meant to work. But still, even with the last solution, there are a variety of problems – and will always be, since we want our design to be as backward compatible as possible (ignoring old browsers is never a good solution).

For example, the second solution will make the text render correctly on IE – but on Mac OS X and iPad Safari it will give birth to another phenomenon: double-bolds and double-italics.

This means that on top of the correct bold and italic, the browser will apply faux ones.

And this is just one of the problems – on a specific OS. But there are sadly more, shared ones on an approach that it widely used, like crashes on some systems and so on.

To be honest, I found the following writing more acceptable, compatible, and with more pros.

So, why didn't I give you it from the start? To illustrate what you'll find more frequently on the net, in tutorials – and the errors that it gives.

I usually prefer to load each font with a different name, with the correct style and weight applied individually.

Yes, I too, hate to have to remember each name – but the "same name family" solution presents some problems on IE (again…) like the fact that you can't apply more than four properties to the same family – this could be forgiven, after all I don't think I will use all the normal, italic, bold, bold-italic styles on the same font on the web (but you never really know) – but this definition makes the browser on the iPad 1 crash 100% of the time too, so…

It's time for a new, better one that is a mix of the above:

```
@font-face {
  font-family: "Cool Font";
  src: url("font.eot");
  src: local(":)"),
    url("font.woff") format("woff"),
    url("font.otf") format("opentype"),
    url("font.svg#filename") format("svg");
  font-weight: 400;
```

```
    font-style: normal;
    }

@font-face {
  font-family: "Cool Font Italic";
  src: url("fontItalic.eot");
  src: local(":)"),
    url("fontItalic.woff") format("woff"),
    url("fontItalic.otf") format("opentype"),
    url("fontItalic.svg#filename") format("svg");
  font-weight: 400;
  font-style: italic;
  }

@font-face {
  font-family: "Cool Font Bold";
  src: url("fontBold.eot");
  src: local(":)"),
    url("fontBold.woff") format("woff"),
    url("fontBold.otf") format("opentype"),
    url("fontBold.svg#filename") format("svg");
  font-weight: 700;
  font-style: normal;
  }
```

Using this method, it's a little bit longer – since you need to address each name separately and to pay attention while setting the exact font-weight, but it's worthy: each style will work perfectly on every browser, even allowing for more than four styles in the same type family in IE.

Doing an extra step and applying the same weight and style in our elements, not only in the @font-face rule, will allow the text to be beautifully styled, even if the desired custom font won't load for any reason, also removing any risk of faux or double styles.

 As of today, if retro compatibility with iPad 1 and older versions on IE is not what you aim for – simply using the Style Linking rule (using the same name for the whole font, directly applying styles and weights to the declaration) will be easier and faster for you.

Font Squirrel and its generator

Now that you have learned how to write your rules by hand, what each property means, and how to locally call for custom fonts it's time to discover one of the more powerful, related websites on the Internet – that will help you with all of the above.

Font Squirrel is a website that provides free fonts for commercial use, getting them from every corner and every type-house on the Internet. (Despite that introduction, I advise you to actually read each font license when you download them from the site, cause their use and allowance may vary.)

Understanding the website and navigating it for desktop purposes is a breeze – and frankly, that's not why we're here talking about it.

We're here to talk about the Web and how Font Squirrel can help us with it – and it's easily explained.

You got one desktop font you love – and you're sure its license allows you to use it online? Great, go on and write your CSS, it's easy and fun.

But what if your loved font only came in .otf or .ttf?

You go up to the website and look: on the right of the navigational menu there is one choice, Generator.

You select the choice you're interested in:

- Basic for straight conversion of the typeface, with minimal compression but no subsetting or anything

- Optimal for a little more work in compression, with automatic removal of missing glyphs, better compression and so on

- And Expert, for which I'm now going to explain the various options:

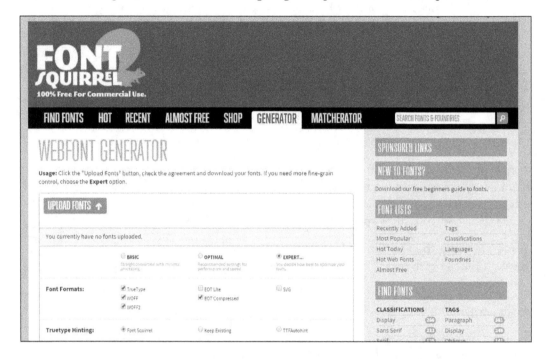

Font Formats explains itself. EOT compressed is the original font with only compression, EOT Lite is the original font stripped of missing glyphs, space and additional features, such as line height.

WOFF2 as we've said, is just a more recent, better compressed version of the original WOFF – but it's very unsupported, so choosing both versions would be the best way.

TrueType Hinting selects the hinting method for the font: calculated by Font Squirrel, the one built into the font (which is sometimes lacking) and one particular source, command-line or standalone built – that's TTFAutohint; built by Werner Lemberg, with help both, financially and supportively, by Google, Microsoft, and many others. It's a software that helps type designers automate the hinting construction for their web fonts – and it's a precise tool. You won't regret choosing this option.

> A later chapter will be dedicated to hinting – a basic explanation of the term is that mathematical instructions for the vector shapes of the characters in a font are used to better align to the raster grid of the screen, making the shapes more readable.

Rendering contains different values as follows:

- **X-height Matching** is a long, technical and boring discourse of which you just need to know the essence. Basically, the inner values inside the sets are the height of the ascenders, depth of the descenders, and the optimal gap between the two in two different lines. This setting makes sure that those values are uniform in every system, making your text act and appear all the same in every system and application. You better check that.

> The vertical values in the fonts you're using are described with three different sets of values: hhea, OS/2 and win – each one of them used by a different OS and application.

- **Gasp table** is a series of instructions that will tell the browser how to render the typeface when seen on grayscale-capable devices. Checking this setting will optimize it across the majority of platforms.

- **Remove kerning** explains itself – and while some fonts are given bad kerning instructions, the vast majority of type designers do nifty work with them, way better than the standard rules that a browser can apply – so you want to leave it unchecked for the font to use its internal set of kerning instructions.

Fix missing glyphs is one kind of subsetting that will remove any blank glyph in the font files, saving space and bandwidth. I dare you not to click them.

X-height matching serves the special purpose of defining the font's x-height to match one of the web safe fonts to avoid any "flashing" while your website loads the custom font; in fact, while this happens, the browser will show your page with standard fonts, like Arial, Courier, Georgia, Times New Roman, Trebuchet, Verdana. After the load the text-affected sections will be refreshed, "jumping or flashing" to the visitor's eye also modifying the page layout, margins, and so on to the ultimate set of design instructions.

Believe me, it sounds worse than it is: there are ways to avoid this with JavaScript and other technologies while using `@font-face`, but they would need another book by themselves.

First you have to learn all the typography terminology and rules, then their applications to the web including the boring, technical stuff like **hhea** (short for **horizontal header**) and so on – after that you still need to master CSS, `@font-face`, and other typography rules and to learn JavaScript. Only then will you be able to encounter this particular topic.

Protection uses HTTP requests, indexes, and referrer checks (meaning you see the actual ID of the incoming request) and other technical data to make sure that the `.ttf` font can't be downloaded from external sources/devices for desktop installation and use.

It works in theory, it's a lot harder in practice – and it can easily be bypassed or get broken meaning that the user won't actually see (in some rare cases) your custom font.

The only true protection for your bought fonts, if you're going to use them on the web, is to actually use only the WOFF and EOT formats.

Subsetting of course offers a no value, a basic one (meaning it will strip your font of everything but Latin characters) and a more complex, user driven option:

Subsetting:	○ Basic Subsetting	● Custom Subsetting...	○ No Subsetting
	Western languages	Custom language support	

Character Encoding:	☐ Mac Roman		

Character Type:	☐ Lowercase	☐ Currency	☐ Lower Accents
	☐ Uppercase	☐ Typographics	☐ Upper Accents
	☐ Numbers	☐ Math Symbols	☐ Diacriticals
	☐ Punctuation	☐ Alt Punctuation	

Language:	☐ Albanian	☐ Faroese	☐ Maltese
	☐ Bosnian	☐ French	☐ Norwegian
	☐ Catalan	☐ Georgian	☐ Polish
	☐ Croatian	☐ German	☐ Portuguese
	☐ Cyrillic	☐ Greek	☐ Romanian
	☐ Czech	☐ Hebrew	☐ Serbian
	☐ Danish	☐ Hungarian	☐ Slovak
	☐ Dutch	☐ Icelandic	☐ Slovenian
	☐ English	☐ Italian	☐ Spanish
	☐ Esperanto	☐ Latvian	☐ Swedish
	☐ Estonian	☐ Lithuanian	☐ Turkish
		☐ Malagasy	

Unicode Tables:	☐ Basic Latin	☐ Punctuation	☐ Latin Extended-B
	☐ Latin-1 Sup	☐ Latin Extended-A	☐ Latin Extended +
	☐ Currency Symbols		

You must know exactly what you're doing here: An error won't be fatal at all, but will make your efforts useless when selecting wrong/empty options. Everything here should be focused toward the audience of your website – so that you can easily eliminate unused languages and characters from the equation.

If your website is aimed at the west – then a basic subsetting will be all you need.

OpenType features is an easy choice: checking the *Keep all features* value will be best – because declaring each option separately will require that you actually know them and how they are named – for example *liga* is usually a subset of every type of ligature, not only the standard ones; and how the subsetting feature specifically works in this very case. So it's easier to keep every feature, including fractions and sups and so on.

OpenType Flatting is really interesting and innovative. Let's say for example you're interested in the built-in, small caps. Sometime, this feature is impossible by web coding – and even CSS3 properties aimed at them sometimes fail, since support of CSS3 is still in progress.

So, if you select this option – and you specifically select it for Small Caps – they will be moved to the lowercase positions allowing you to obtain one web font specifically usable for small caps. (Of course, what's valid for small caps is valid for all the other available features)

Please keep in mind this is to be used as a second passage – firstly save the web font in a regular style, so that you can use lowercase – and do this particular selection in a second instance, saving two separate files for two different uses of the same font. Otherwise you'll risk losing some basic, needed features.

CSS, of course, refers to the stylesheet creation and to three basic properties of it, one being its name:

- Base64 is a binary-to-text conversion that represents the usual binary values in some ASCII text inside your CSS. Basically, when everything else fails for the browser in loading your font externally (may it be a firewall, or an alien invasion) this will step-in and visualize your font everywhere.

- One understandable drawback is the fact that it adds a lot of weight to your CSS – so the best solution remains using it as a standalone property in a separate CSS file to be called after all others.

- Style link of course is the norm of naming each font-family the same for different weights and styles, as explained earlier. It is your choice to keep it or leave it, whatever you prefer to work with – earlier we discussed pros and cons of every approach in painstaking detail.

Advanced options are quite a thing: I usually remove the -webfont name suffix, as I prefer my type names shorter; other options are better left as standard, especially the **Em Square Value**.

Shortcuts explain itself: are you going to do any heavy use of this website and features now that I have explained it to you?

Of course you are! It's so useful, it's inexplicable!

But are you completely sure the setting you're using for this font is optimal for the next time you visit it with a completely different font? It's better to leave it unchecked.

Agreement is important, as you're telling the website owner and runner that you know that the license for the font you're submitting allows you to use the fonts on the web and to modify their original values.

What it doesn't say is that if the license doesn't allow it, you're committing a crime for which (rightfully so) you're responsible, not Font Squirrel and the type maker and original owner will search for solutions, sometimes monetary ones, directly to you, the owner of the website where the fraud has been perpetrated.

So don't check it light-heartedly – and always read the EULA.

And now what?

Now it's time for you to download your package (a button will appear, after the correct upload of the file, in the lower-right); click that button and every necessary transformation will happen in a matter of minutes, if not seconds.

Then you'll download your `.zip` file, containing an `.html` example page, every selected format – and your `.css` file, where you can copy the values to the one for your website giving birth to the magic implementation of self-hosted, CSS custom fonts – for free!

To close the free instrument chapters: there are quite a few handy tools. So why did we only concentrate on Font Squirrel? It's not like they pay us to name-drop them. I wish they did (would have meant more money for me).

Simply, it's the best free tool available out there – always up to date; it's even been the first to adopt the best, more correct, and least problematic solutions every time they came out. Like Paul Irish's smiley, correct syntaxes, or anything else – always giving birth to the best CSS `@font-face` declarations for the end user.

So it's completely useless to look at other sources – if you own the font and you're looking for local-hosting, that's the tool for you.

Google web fonts

It's a free, great \service for the people who want an easier job than all the above – and a little faster too, since font files are hosted on Google servers.

Each font is free for commercial use – and you can download them for desktop usage too (Google did all the homework for you).

Of course, the choices available aren't premium like the typefaces you can purchase for hundreds of dollars – but if you're on a budget, choosing from it's huge library (703 families and counting!) is a great thing to do.

Its use is simple:

1. Open `https://www.google.com/fonts`.

2. Select the family you want, with the help of the filters on the window's left.

3. When you click on the font you like, the window will enlarge showing you new buttons on the lower-right.

4. Clicking the **Pop out** one will allow you to focus more on the font at first, to see some statistics about its usage (country, number of downloads, and so on) and more importantly, in the **Pairings** tab you'll be able to see some pre-made pairings of it with other fonts in the library. A lot of them will be boring and useless, but sometimes you'll encounter some beautiful couplings that it's best to take note of.

5. After all that info, you can click on **Use** and a new window will open, with a lot of possibilities to select from.

You can select the different weights and styles for your family – with a widget on the right that will tell you exactly how much every additional style will slow down your website load time (little hint: you want to keep them to a minimum.)

Choosing the character sets is simply automatic subsetting – it's up to you.

The third step is integration with your website.

You'll want to add the first link, CSS into the `<head>` section of your page – it will look something like this:

```
<link href='https://fonts.googleapis.com/css?family=Name'
    rel='stylesheet' type='text/css'
```

That's it, you're done!

Actual CSS integration with your website is as simple as setting the font-family value for your element with the exact font name (Google will give you that under the CSS link) – really, nothing else is needed!

If you need to use multiple typefaces, from the selection window, click on the blue **Add to collection** button: this will make a little bar on the bottom of the browser window.

On the same bar, click on **Use** and you'll be brought to the exact same page as before – where CSS is given.

This time it will feature two or multiple families, each one divided by a | character.

```
<link href='https://fonts.googleapis.com/css?family=Name1|Name2'
    rel='stylesheet' type='text/css'>
```

Recall the different names in different elements in your CSS and everything is set.

Each font will have a standard behavior, meaning that you'll be able to apply all the CSS properties we've studied in the previous chapters.

And while Google Fonts lacks some particular, specific characterization that you're able to get only with self-hosted fonts (such as specific subsetting, font flattening, hinting and more) when talking about CSS they recently added the possibility to apply some beautiful things to their fonts, like flame aspects, wallpaper, or steel visuals.

To use them on every instance of the font, just add the following to your Google CSS link, where `effect-name` has to be substituted with the actual effect:

```
&effect=effect-name
```

A complete list of them is visible at the following URL:

```
https://developers.google.com/fonts/docs/getting_started#Effects
```

What I truly advise is not to blindly apply them, but to study each one, and how they are obtained: you'll see they're nothing more than basic CSS rules applied by professionals. And what separate you from a professional of that level is just the time and passion applied.

Time for a couple of paid services

After talking about free options, self- and remote-hosted, it's time to spend a few words on just a couple of paid services – and why you'd want to use them.

Keep in mind our selection has to be limited – otherwise taking into account every paid service at this moment will need a separate book, since almost every type-foundry and vendor allows some type of separate, local- or remote-hosted service.

We made our choice based on popularity, longevity, and typeface selection.

So let's start, without a particular order.

Typekit

A real revolutionary service, Typekit has explored the typography possibilities on the web since September 2009; the very first service and idea of this type, beating Google by many, many months. It has used `@font-face` since the beginning, using JavaScript to insert the CSS in your website and to work around performance.

Of course in six years, and after Adobe's acquisition in 2011 things have changed and evolved, but the base is still there.

What's different from using the `@font-face` rule yourself is the fact that it is a hosted service: you won't buy one font and put its files on your server – you'll buy a subscription (monthly, yearly, whatever you prefer) and gain instant, remote access (via their interface) to more than 1,100 type families (actual Adobe official data).

Try putting them on your server – you'll probably make it crash irreparably and get kicked out by your hosting company.

Pricing varies from the free plan, with access to 800+ fonts per 25,000 page views per month, only two fonts at the same time on one website – to huge business plans of $400 with 25M visitors per month.

If the free plan is too limiting for you, you can pay as little as $49 per month to access the entire 4200+ font library for 500,000 page views per month on unlimited websites.

 With the acquisition by Adobe, it now allows you to synchronize and use the library fonts on desktop software like Creative Cloud and Office, for example. But we won't investigate that here.

After all this information, let's explain how to use it for your website.

Of course, we always start with selecting our desired typefaces – with such a wide selection, things can get messy pretty easily – and you can find you spent the whole working day just looking at fonts.

Congrats, no payday for you.

Hey, let's not joke here – I personally love spending days in front of fonts – and if you have bought (or illegally downloaded this book) I think you do too!

So start scavenging! Luckily, Adobe made it easier for us, with selectors for family type and for characteristics such as width, contrast, weight, and so on.

Two custom proprietary lists are Headings and Paragraphs, with handmade selected fonts by the staff. Mixing every value in this area will help you a lot in aiming for the perfect font for your project.

There is also a collection and special filters for Japanese only fonts which will come in handy from project to project.

Ok, after you select the fonts, you click on them, click on the green bottom of the neat popup coming in.

After the popup, you'll be prompted with a new popup that will tell you to **Create a Kit**, which is nothing more than a virtual folder containing one or more projects with different domains in which you can add the different fonts you need, as per the following image:

Select the **Web** tab.

You'll be prompted to click on **Create a kit**; give it a name and the domain.

You'll then be given basic JavaScript to be added into the <head> of your page, something like this:

```
<script src="https://use.typekit.net/wgg3dss.js"></script>
<script>try{Typekit.load({ async: true });}catch(e){}</script>
```

It works by blocking rendering of the page while first loading the font, so it does not show the flashing of the page when the new custom font loads in, like we talked about a little earlier.

Clicking on **Continue** will let you enter the world of that font, with the possibility of specifying selectors for the appliance of it, language subsetting, openType features (to keep 'em or not), weights and styles; every time updating the weight of your final file at the bottom.

When you hit **Publish**, if you added the JS code to the head of your document – nothing will happen. Nothing for the first couple of minutes, then bursts of joy will wander through your heart as with a little refresh – your page has magical loaded the new font.

Apart from the ease of use, the variety of beautifully designed, and web-specific typefaces – what's great about Typekit is what lies underneath: they're always up to date with the latest technologies to render type beautifully even to the smallest detail; using a mixture of the **DirectWrite** rendering engine, **PostScript** outlines with Grayscale antialiasing, for example, and smoothed at the largest sizes, some display typefaces like Bello Pro.

Are you having a headache right now? It's all part of hinting, which will be evaluated later. Just so you know, this is one of the different mixtures they apply to be sure that type renders perfectly on the screen – just one. Does it mean they apply it to the whole library and call it a day?

Not these guys. They mix and match selectively for some typefaces – then redo the work for other typefaces. Always on the run for the latest tricks, what does it mean for you, the end-user?

Will this complicate your time behind your website, chasing for that last button, the last optimized bit on the site – since the previous one made it crash? Wouldn't be a worry, would it?

Again, the guys do all the work, all the testing – on every typeface. You'll just have to click that **Publish** button from time to time and that's it.

If you don't want to buy every single font you'll ever need, store them locally and write CSS by hand, with the risk of it being ignored by some browsers – go to these guys, they know their job extremely well.

Cloud typography

If we're talking about typography, we cannot talk about Hoefler & Co. – sadly, previously known as Hoefler & Frere-Jones 'til January 16 2014 –this world of beautiful words was shattered from the ground up because Tobias Frere-Jones filed a lawsuit against Jonathon Hoefler, marking the division of one of the most beautiful places for typography in the entire world – and filling many of our eyes with tears.

The company sits at the base of what are some of the most beautiful typefaces ever created: Gotham, Tungsten, Whitney, Verlag, Sentinel and so on

For the new medium, since each of those little masterpieces was made for print – they took them, redesigned them, and refined them for screen, each one.

Thanks to that, our websites can look beautiful as never before – let's take a look at how to use the service.

Subscriptions here are based purely on page views – unlimited website usage.

You can start with $99 per year per 250,000 page views and add from there.

Once you purchase and log in, you'll also find that the account keeps a memory of every font you purchase from them for desktop usage – so if you lose the files locally, you won't have much trouble in downloading them again.

Also, if you're paying for the cloud plan, with every desktop purchase you obtain the same font for Web usage absolutely free.

There's a big drawback that I see as a huge defect in the working process: you pay your yearly fee for page views, including unlimited websites, but you still have to purchase one-off web licenses for each font.

When looking around at all those breathtaking, huge quality fonts, you'll see a "web-only" small price that you'll be able to purchase for instant usage on the web.

Sincerely, I highly prefer the "pay once, access the entire library" feature of Typekit.

Anyway, upon registering, Hoefler & Co. give you five web fonts for free – so make those choices count.

To start using them, you'll need to create a so-called project: an ensemble of web fonts that will work on the domains you'll enter under the Welcome screen.

Each project needs a name, a domain and a first font to start – you'll be able to change those values anytime – and to add domains to the same project later.

You can have a maximum of 10 active projects at a time – which basically means 10 different sets of font combinations on unlimited domains; you can add them by paying one additional dollar per month per additional project.

[One thing to pay attention to: your page view count will start from the day of the purchase and will reset each month.]

But since there are two modes in which you can work on project, you need to be careful and to learn the differences before starting to work with them:

- **Development** is for building and testing your project – you can try and visualize the chosen combo online without using any of your monthly pages (instead you're using part of your one GB of development bandwidth allowed.).

- **Production** is the final step in your work: while entering this mode the fonts will be moved and applied to your websites/domains selected and you'll start using your monthly page views.

What's behind the curtain with your project is a Delivery Agent: an application that runs on more than 125,000 worldwide servers (so it's unlikely it will ever stop working due to a crash of all of them) that will identify the visitor request as: which website it is directed to, which project it is related to, and which OS and browser it is using. It will then deliver the very perfect file type for that specific request.

All in an instant – you won't even notice it's there.

Ok, apart from pushing a couple of buttons – to create a project and run from development to production – how do you actually integrate the fonts in your design?

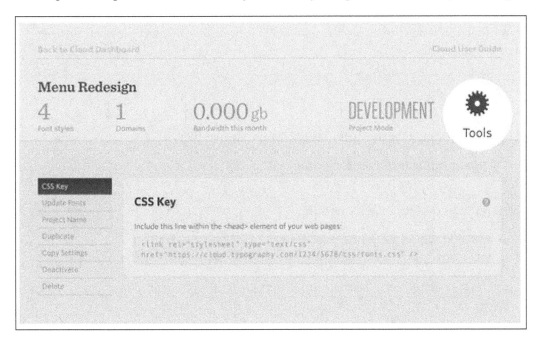

In tools on the top you'll find the CSS Key: just copy that small snippet of text – which looks something like this:

```
<link rel="stylesheet" type="text/css" href="//cloud.typography.
com/1234/5678/css/fonts.css" />
```

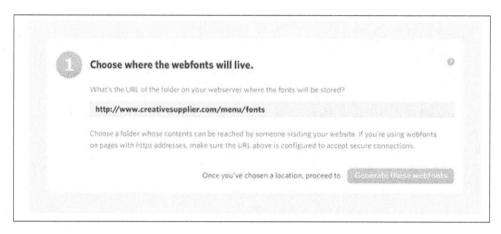

Paste it in your document `<head>` (before any other stylesheet) and the Agent will take care of the rest.

After that you'll need to apply the usual CSS font-family property to your desired elements, like this:

```
font-family: " Text A", "Text B";
font-weight: 400;
font-style: normal;
```

It's worth noticing that they divide each font into two files, to:

> [...] prevent misuse of the files – Hoefler Staff

Let me translate that: you won't be easily downloading their web fonts and using them on your desktop like it's nothing.

And how that would even be a possibility?

Contrary to popular belief, cloud typography is a self-hosted font service. Despite the cloud contained in the name, that part only applies to the Agent.

Yes, after you push the Publish button you'll be prompted to enter a path – on your server – for the service to move the font files.

So, after all, you're paying the subscription cost to possibly select, and additionally pay for, their splendid fonts – but you'll have to use your own space and bandwidth.

Other inside features are standard for this kind of service, like the selection of special, OpenType features.

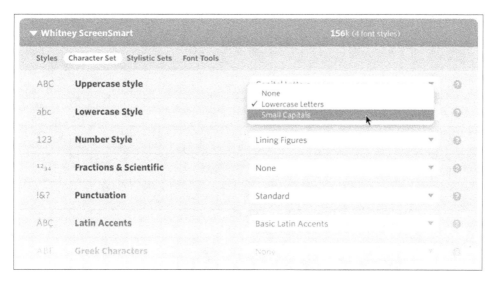

In conclusion, it's a service that is indeed useful – but only if you are really aiming for the Hoefler & Co. typefaces.

A small tip about CT rendering: despite all the promises, the use of an advanced selector application that should deliver the exact font file for every situation, and the base redesign and refinement of a lot of typefaces in their library (you'll notice them by the addition of the cool ScreenSmart suffix in the name), rendering of the fonts is not as cool as it could be.

The following is the screen you'll be welcomed with on the **Cloud.typography** service – with the real application, it is a functional preview of their fonts; Tungsten and Whitney:

Tungsten clearly suffers some antialiasing problems, especially on curves – but sometimes even straight lines. (All these screenshots are taken from the Cloud typography's own pages while writing this chapter on my Windows PC from a variety of browsers all in their latest release.)

BEHIND THE SCENES

The Delivery Agent

To deliver browser-specific fonts without any database calls, Cloud.typography custom builds an autonomous DELIVERY AGENT that runs in the cloud.

Even the Sentinel font suffers from antialiasing problems, more noticeably than Tungsten.

It's a picky detail, but one that we hope will be resolved in the future service updates.

Still, to use Hoefler & Co.'s own typefaces, there is no other way so you'll find yourself jumping on board. Despite every shady feature and function, (shady because it takes time to understand what the limits are, how they work, and so on) and forgetting everything else when you see how beautiful their fonts are, they will make your website look beautiful.

Summary

Within this chapter we learned the free and paid services for better looking web-fonts, their pros and cons, how to implement them in detail, and each web font format and their implementation differences.

Despite this, you may want to remember that the Internet is crawling with web-font services to the point that almost every foundry has a specific one so to analyze every one of them with their requirements and features would take a hundred pages.

Since it's not what we're doing here, we had to limit ourselves – by time of existence, number, and precision of its features and variety of fonts.

Being the real pioneer – and at the same time, the best innovator in the field, our choice couldn't have been anything else other than Typekit – but remember there are a myriad of other services, like the one offered by `https://www.fonts.com/web-fonts` or `http://www.webtype.com/`, `http://fontdeck.com/` and many, many more. There was even one from the Android Droid typeface makers – that sadly is not working anymore. There are too many to actually list them here.

We then chose to review and explain Cloud typography because of the exclusive typefaces and because of its popularity (which despite that, has some flaws that we're sure will be addressed in the future).

So please, don't limit yourself to the content of this chapter, go out there and explore. The Internet is vast and beautiful; the perfect solution for your typography needs is just waiting for you.

4
Modern Scale

Within this chapter you're going to learn how to practically balance your text with well proportioned titles, subtitles, and more.

Very simple math will be required – but don't worry, it will be explained step-by-step. We are going to move through:

- What is a scale?
- How to find its numbers?
- How to apply them with CSS?
- Defining vertical rhythm

We will also make a more complex, responsive structure – mixing the notions of the previous chapter with the upcoming ones.

So, what are we waiting for? Let's start!

What is a font scale?

Good looking fonts alone won't necessarily make a beautiful, well balanced design.

We'll need a little math to step in to help us so that we'll be able to build a report of values between each element of our text– for it to appear harmonious, rhythmical, and more readable.

We need to define a **scale**.

You may not know it – but you look and use the classic typographic scale every time you fire up Adobe InDesign, Microsoft Word, or any modern software: the standard point sizes that are given to you are just that.

In a scale, each element answers to the scaling property, meaning that where x is a value, rx or it's ratio must be present inside the scale as well.

That ratio element is the foundation of the scale – and it's the numeric value we are going to work on.

The classic typographic scale is made of these values: 6, 7, 8, 9, 10, 11, 12, 14, 16, 18, 21, 24, 36, 48, 60, 72. You recognize it now, don't you?

Another important property of a scale is the number of the notes. Each interval of the classic one encloses five sizes, making it a pentatonic scale.

The last important thing is the frequency – in the classic typographic scale this value is the pica – which is a type unit of measure consisting of 12 points, invented by François-Ambroise Didot in 1785.

It's the baseline value for print, where basic readable text is set at 12 points – the equivalent of 1 pica.

Using a classic formula for the frequency f of every note i as shown in the following image:

$$f_i = f_0 r^{\frac{i}{n}}$$

We can find out that the classic typographic scale is missing or has misplaced some values: 28, 32, 42 and 55 measures are missing – while 60 and 72 should be 63 and 73 points, to keep the scale on the same frequency.

Probably the values were rounded up to the closest pica multiple value to be easier to use and apply in the old print world. As a final tip, the 11 value doesn't really belong there, thanks to the formula.

Ok, so we learned that the **classic typography scale** that we've been applying for years is wrong. Don't worry, this won't turn the world upside down, not even the typographical one.

It's more of a general wrongness, given by limitations of the times when it was created. Keep using it with ease; it won't do any damage to your text or your ability to read it easily, the eye and general knowledge have grown used to it during the centuries.

Creating a new scale

As we know, the web is a different medium from print: different resolution, different reading and writing rules.

Let's see how all of the above easily fit the new medium as well.

There are three methods to change and build a scale – each one is based on the variation of its basic properties. You can change the frequency, adapting an existing scale to a new project. For example, frequency=12pt is the print medium, while frequency=16pt is the web medium. By changing the number of values, you can have more sizes available for your project – but it is not really needed. After all, who needs more than three/four sizes in a real world, text based project?

The third solution – and maybe the more interesting – is to change the ratio of the scale, giving birth to other, completely different values inside it.

Let's start out by defining a scale for the web with one of the most eye pleasing measures you'll find out there: the Golden Ratio. Also known as **Phi (Φ)**, it's an irrational number usually presented as 1.618

To obtain a scale, we must decide a base number to start with. Written content for the web is usually advisable to be written starting from 16 points and up.

 The common distance at which we sit from a screen is from 20 to 23 inches (recommended 28"). The optimal readability at this distance, given all factors – like the light that enters the eye, convergence, words per sentence – is mathematically given by a measure of 16pt on the screen. This is why it's the standard size.

As such, browser makers around the world adopted the 16 points as a standard on their software – which in modern type is found, named, and referable to as 1em.

What is an em?

While not completely related to our Phi explanation and exercise, (we'll be back to that soon, I promise,) explaining ems is absolutely relevant to typography and especially, to responsive typography.

In the old times of manual typesetting, the line-height of the physical block that the letter was built upon was the em. This gave birth to the element knowledge and arbitrary measure of it. Yes, it's arbitrary because it varies from font to font, usually being defined as the width of the capital M (hence the em name,) since the M usually fulfilled the casted blocks width. One em was equal to the current point size – so 1em generically equals 1pt.

In CSS, the em is equal to the height of the font. Since a standard needed to be developed for all browser rules and rendering options, 1em lost its arbitrary measure, being equal to a readable standard of 16pt for the screen. Height still varies depending on the font being used, but writing 1em without any user specific declaration will always mean 16pt, despite the font.

In fact, you can define the em rule as any other: if you apply the font-size for every written part in the body selector through a percentage or number, you'll modify the standard behavior: for example a declaration like this one:

```
body { font-size: 62,5%; }
```

This will reduce and render the 16pt em to 10pt as a regular measure. If you specify later in the CSS, your elements as 1em – they will be rendered at 10px.

Why are ems important?

An em is a worldwide standard, defining the 16pt value. But within your project, they easily turn into relative values, referring to the defined measure in your document.

Acting on just the containing element, their use in responsive design is really a must: whatever method you use to resize the website content, just defining again the base in your breakpoint will make all the successive elements resize accordingly.

Pixel values on the other hand, being fixed, allow a better, more precise control on the design. But as I said they are fixed: they aren't relative to any element: If you want them to scale for the mobile viewer, you'll have to define each element again.

Let's also not forget the fact that older IE browsers (IE8 for example) didn't allow any liberty to the user, you were unable to scale fonts through the Text Size tool - only with zooming, which is clearly another thing – and certainly unwanted behavior.

Defect in the em element

Despite being relative font sizing values, problems in the standard submission and implementation made it act quite variedly: while the idea was good, the implementation lacked something here and there, making it a contextual element.

It simply means, unfortunately, that the original em behavior has been shifted: not only referring to the base element, it now calls and scale accordingly to its container element.

Here we define a body element of 100% or 1em:

```
p { font-size: 0.625em }
```

This will act normally, being rendered at 10px.

But if our p is wrapped inside an article, it will act contextually: meaning it will still be rendered at `0.625em` – but according to the px size of the article itself, not longer of the base element and measure set in our page. This little defect means more math for us – and a less-straightforward implementation, since in responsive, we may need to change more than one value. Still, since its launch, this element has been more powerful and adjustable than the pixel defined size.

The CSS3 solution

Since these element problems, or better, unwanted behavior, became known, the geniuses at the W3C worked hard and with the CSS3 specification they evolved and rewrote the em element again. To not cause harm to the innumerable tons of websites coded with the previous specification, they re-released it as a new element, called rem.

Rem stands for **Root em**, specifying that the element and sizing is indeed tied to the root of your document. No more contextual behavior, no more inherited sizing: every font-size expressed in rems will be resized accordingly to the HTML or body specified one.

To calculate a rem element is simpler: you won't have to remember every container and their sizes- you'll just define the base, divide the next desired values by that and you're good to go!

Let's see an example:

```
Body { font-size:1em; }
```

As we know, 1em is equal to 16px. So, having decided, for example, our primary header will be 32px high, the transformation in rems is quite simple:

32 / 16 = 2 or 2rem

We'll just have to write down the following:

```
h1 { font-size: 2rem; }
```

Our header is now the desired size.

But what if the h1 is contained, let's say, in an article, which we forgot that we set to 0.625rem, clearly referring to the standard text in it and not to the headers?

Well that's a no-brainer and not a problem, since rems will always refer only to the root defined measure – and not to the above element. Our header will act and render as expected.

What to expect from rems?

Surely, this element is a dream for every web designer – but like every latest release, it's only supported by more modern browsers and onward – past ones will act weird on things they don't understand.

The simpler solution is to implement rems in your project – and provide a fallback measure by giving a second, pixel set declaration in the same element.

All abroad the rems train! Woot woot!

Time to get back to the scale

So, why the long run off-topic on elements and their definitions?

Because talking more about responsive typography, no longer about typography itself is a talk that was really needed. Now you know the basic differences between pixels, ems and rems – and from now on I'll be writing code and text size for the web in rem units. This will of course affect our math on scales too, so our little essay was mandatory.

As we said earlier, web type is usually seen as a standard of 16px – and the Golden Ratio is a number close and expressible as 1.618. So, how we can mix the two numbers together – to achieve rhythm and flow in our text, using a scale? This requires a little math for every element we're going to need. As we've seen, general text usually requires three levels – so we'll need at least three elements.

Let's add a fourth, in case a subtitle or a small paragraph of explanation of a footer of some sort is needed:

1. We'll start with the basic text, which will be a standard, well readable 16px.

2. How do we obtain one header that will be in harmony with our text? We choose our ratio, a Golden one actually, so let's apply it to our text value:

    *16 * 1.618 = 25.8888*

    We'll adjust it accordingly to 25.9px

3. Now we'll need to transform it to rem – so a division per our base element will be needed.

4. After the first arithmetical operation, we'll find that our h2 is 1.6 times our text, so

    ```
    h2 { font-size: 1.6rem; }
    ```

5. Easy, isn't it? Now onto our first level, or `h1`.

6. Since the modular scale, we'll need to multiply our last value for our ratio to obtain the next value:

    *25.9 * 1.1618 = 41.9px*

    That translated into rems is:

    41.9 / 16 = 2.6rem

    so:

    h1 { font-size: 2.6rem; }

7. We'll need a bigger element? No problem, we'll take our last value and multiply it by our ratio. A smaller one? We'll take our last value and divide it by our ratio.

8. After that, it's time to take every value and divide it per our baseline – and we have a rhythmical, easy to apply and visually appealing typographic scale.

Let's apply it to our previous example/exercise poem and look at the differences, shall we?

Nothing but Death

PABLO NERUDA - 1926

There are cemeteries that are lonely,

graves full of bones that do not make a sound

the heart moving through a tunnel

in it darkness, darkness, darkness

like a shipwreck we die going into ourselves

as though we were drowning inside our hearts

as though we lived falling out of the skin into the soul

While the design and proportions are pleasant enough, the H2 is almost as big as the H1, apparently. Did we break the Golden Ratio? Is such a rule non-existent? Did I do something wrong?

Reality is that every scale, every design – has to be tested on the field – and every scale, every rule, has to be applied to the specific project. In this case, our font selection of a sans with a higher x-height than our serif almost nullifies the hierarchy of our document. Applying the same font as the rest with the same letter-spacing looks and feels completely different:

Nothing but Death

Pablo Neruda - 1926

There are cemeteries that are lonely,

graves full of bones that do not make a sound

the heart moving through a tunnel

in it darkness, darkness, darkness

like a shipwreck we die going into ourselves

as though we were drowning inside our hearts

as though we lived falling out of the skin into the soul

Our hierarchy is better defined and reliable – and more pleasant to the eye.

We'll just have to select a different typeface for the second level and we'll be good – or, another meaningful solution would be to select a smaller-than text value, like the design we achieved in our first exercise. After all, the subtitle is less important than our text, so it would be a good solution too.

You may encounter some huge gaps from value to value – this will be explored next. Hopefully this example taught you a good lesson on web design: even when everything has been settled up and seems perfect, always test it many times before launching your project to the public or sending it to the client.

Believe me, it's a valuable lesson. So, we have just seen a simple calculus of a scale to apply it to our design: while useful and interesting, is it all there? There is actually more – more complicated things when writing and applying code and a scale for a responsive design. And we're now going to take a look at it.

A more complex exercise

Since this exercise will be more complex, we will bring the application of a modular scale, forward from our little beginning. We'll do our best to maintain at least the same initial values, so some math has already been covered. We are going to make a responsive structure out of rems.

Vertical rhythm

We have talked about rhythm for quite some time, it's time for a little pause in the exercise aimed at a better study of it. VR in text should be a strong, regular, repeated pattern of words and sounds. It's harder than it sounds. Keeping it consistent enough on our webpage will define a more readable, relaxing experience. In this specific case, the majority of the work is up to font-size and line-height.

 Another important thing to have is a consistent baseline: One general rule, apart from the print one of having the line-height at 120% of the font – is to have it for the web at 140/160%.

Right in the middle sits 1.5 – which seems a comfortable, easy to implement value, since having a base of 100% (16px) for our text, the line height will translate perfectly to 24px. Starting from there, we must make sure that every margin, text, padding, and so on just adds up to that measure.

For example – if you have one element you want with less space on top and more on the bottom, this code will keep it on the baseline initially defined:

```
p.subtle { font-size: 1rem;
line height: 1.5rem;
margin: 1rem 0.75rem 0.5rem 0.75rem;
}
```

Yes, it's simple and believe me – it works. It can be done by dividing multiples too, since our example will probably be too restricted. But who cares? We're experimenting, and experimenting should be fun and a travel into the unknown at first: we'll have time to refine and define later.

To be fair, we should already have been applying **single-direction margins**, which are a genius way to maintain vertical rhythm: since in this case we'll be probably moving each element downward, applying a margin-bottom to any of our block elements will make sure that, every time we create a new element and drop it on the page, it will fall exactly at the same distance from the rest, keeping the baseline intact:

```
h1,h2,h3,h4,h5,h6,hgroup,
ul,ol,dd,p,figure,
pre,table,fieldset,hr { margin-bottom:1.5rem; }
```

Quite a time saver, huh? The same can be done and calculated for left/right margins too. Working with images is quite easy as well: we have the value, we just need their heights to be a multiple of that – and to add the same bottom-margin.

For example, we scale one image to 240px (*24 * 10*) and have the standard 1.5rem bottom-margin.

Or if the image is longer and we don't want to cut it, let's say 252px – we can add a smaller bottom margin of 12px/0.75 rem and still being alright! This will also fix the collapsing-margins issue, so why not use it?

The collapsing-margin issue usually happens when two vertical margins are next to each other – and the browser applies only the greater one of the two, leaving your design not exactly the way you wanted it.

It can also happen when the parent element margin overrides the child vertical margin, keeping only its own one.

Ok, now we know how to basically maintain vertical rhythm through our design. What about our scale?

Time to get back to it.

We already have some values for our text – 1, 1.6, 2.6 rems and now we have found out about our margins, which are 1.5 rem. Let's explain another thing about scales in general: if we want our design to be based on them, we won't use them only for our text and their hierarchies: we'll use our values, in different and sometimes in random ways until we think it's right – on every part of our design. This includes margins, paddings, widths, blank spaces, and so on. So, it does look like four values are not enough for our project. Luckily, enlarging the scale is simple: we just take the last values and divide/multiply them as needed.

This will allow us to use more values, as 4.2, 0.6, 0.3 rems. So our scale now looks like this: *0.3 – 0.6 – 1 – 1.6 – 2.6 – 4.2 – 6.8 – 11.*

Way more useful already. But what if the progression and the numbers were unforgiving? What if we needed more values? What if we don't want to achieve the beautiful mess it produced above with our poem, due to the similarities in our values and fonts?

The solution would have been to work on a double-stranded scale, which means that will be two starting point values or two different ratios mixed up to enlarge our possibilities – in just one scale.

 Making sure that at least the starting point or the ratio, stay the same – will assure us of the balance and harmony of the exiting values.

To choose the second value, you should find something that's important and related to your project – and that is different enough from the first value.

Now, let's imagine we're working on a responsive website – and that we sketched it out on paper. Let's imagine our base structure being composed of six columns, for a maximum width of the layout to the standard 1140px measure.

Dividing it by 6, the number of our columns, we find out the 190px value - so we could have used that for our double-stranded scale.

The math from there would have been simple enough to obtain the rest of the values. We know the numbers, we know the ratio, it's just the boring job of divisions and multiplications – and after that it's time to convert them to rems, keeping in mind that our base value has always been 16 – so each number should have been divided by that very one number.

But luckily, as of today we can save some time and headaches in our project by going on the wonderful website that is: `http://www.modularscale.com/`. insert our values, finding the remaining ones to fulfill our double stranded scale.

Keep the double-stranded scale in mind, it will surely turn out useful in the future. Right now we're just in need of knowing our 190px as rems – and it's simple as:

190 / 16 = 11.875

All that's left now is to define a basic page structure, apply the rems value to it and use some fictional text to fill it up and test it inside our browsers:

```
body { font-size: 100%; }
.column #1    {    width: 11.875rem; }
.column #2    {    width: 23.75rem; }
.column #3    {    width: 35.625rem; }
.column #4    {    width: 47.5rem; }
.column #5    {    width: 59.375rem; }
.column #6    {    width: 71.25rem; }
```

The result we expect from the above is something like this:

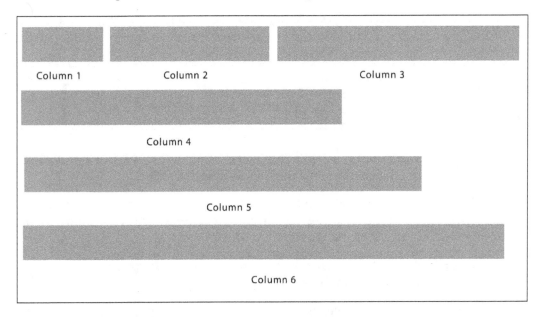

This will define our basic page structure. You'll simply find out that our column six will cover the entire 1140px grid, being 71.25 rems the value of 1140 on a 16px base.

```
h1 { font-size: 4.2rem; }
h2 { font-size: 2.6rem; }
h3 { font-size: 1.6rem; }
p { font-size: 1rem; }
.footer { font-size: 0.6rem; }
```

We will then add basic properties to our columns to float – and a little padding:

```
.column { float: left;
padding: 1em 0 0 1em; }
```

Adding a little container for our content with little-to-no basic properties and some text – with the first column one being shorter in width, otherwise it will break the small width column, (despite the break-word property applied owing to the difference in rems,) will result in something like this on the web:

Short

Lorem

Lorem Ipsum is simply dummy text of the printing and typesetting industry. Lorem Ipsum has been the industry's standard dummy text ever since the 1500s, when an unknown printer took a galley of type and scrambled it to make a type specimen book. It has survived not only five centuries, but also the leap into electronic typesetting, remaining essentially unchanged. It was popularised in the 1960s with the release of Letraset sheets containing Lorem Ipsum passages, and more recently with desktop publishing software like Aldus PageMaker including versions of Lorem Ipsum.

Longer Lorem Ipsum than h2

Lorem Ipsum

Lorem Ipsum is simply dummy text of the printing and typesetting industry. Lorem Ipsum has been the industry's standard dummy text ever since the 1500s, when an unknown printer took a galley of type and scrambled it to make a type specimen book. It has survived not only five centuries, but also the leap into electronic typesetting, remaining essentially unchanged. It was popularised in the 1960s with the release of Letraset sheets containing Lorem Ipsum passages, and more recently with desktop publishing software like Aldus PageMaker including versions of Lorem Ipsum.

As you can see, everything is there and is well balanced to the eye. Of course, fine tuning is needed in removing the base applied margins to H2, applying line-height, and so on.

Balancing a text block always needs a lot of trial and error. Keep in mind to check the overall density of the paragraphs and the readability of the text, through line height and width of the column.

 Just remember where you started: if you have a baseline set (and you should) – keep it consistent throughout the design. Add it in one go (single-direction margins) or split it up.

To wrap up this modular scale lesson, remember one important thing: they're just a tool, nothing is mandatory. Using them with the values you like is efficient, time-saving – and beautiful. If you start using them today it will make your text and structure well balanced, rhythmical, and harmonious for sure. But they are nothing more than guides. They are no substitute for your eyes and experience.

If there are numbers you feel are better than the ones provided by the scale, (for example, H2) use them without feeling ashamed about it. Or if you want, you can use a **double-stranded** scale, or you can combine the values that are already present, to get close to the desired one.

This approach basically transforms the way you work with the web: content and type will define the structure, instead of the contrary – and they will be really tied together. Without your specific font and your specific font size, structure will become meaningless. So, remember to always provide pixel measures and default font line-height and margins as a fall-back, in case any problems with the loading of your font arises.

A little note on ems and rems

You surely noted that our structure is not built by pixel, but in relation to text. This makes content – and typography – king. Writing structures and columns by ems allows us to always provide the best reading experience as possible, in width of the sentence and in number of characters. This approach has never been possible through the pixel-fixed layout.

As everything is built to a relative size, if we zoom in or out from our page, font-size will change. In pixel size this would mean complete changes in paragraph widths and readability – while with ems any change to the font size will keep readability at its best, with always the optimal line length.

A game changer indeed!

Summary

Within this chapter we learnt what a typographic scale is, why your software always lists the same point values for typographic approaches, what relative values are, and how to use them.

We also learnt how to make a completely responsive structure out of them – so it's been kind of a long run.

Take some rest now, because in the next chapter we are going to see how to tie element measures to the screen size.

Viewport and Size

5

In the next couple of chapters, we'll explore other solutions to achieve the perfect responsive design for your project, mixing and matching them with the previous tips and tricks.

We'll start with a way to dynamically resize your content — and especially your type of course — based on the visible area of your screen.

As we'll see, this one is quite different for the rest of the solutions out there — in both good and bad aspects.

We'll start with explaining what the viewport actually is, and then we will move on to how to operate in it with CSS3 using custom tailored measures.

Are you ready? Let's start!

The viewport concept

First, we need to understand one simple thing: the visible area of the screen, which is called **viewport**. Of course, it varies from device to device, and obviously, working with measures directly related and strictly linked to it seems like a good idea.

Its first widespread notion and implementation came with the introduction of HTML5 standard, which added a `<meta>` tag specifically for it.

Metadata is information about the data on the page. It is usually related to language, SEO aspects, and description of the content among other things. While not clearly visible on the page, this data is read and used by machines — they always are inside the head element.

The metadata viewport is expressed by the name (`="viewport"`), the width property, and the initial-scale of one.

Of course, those properties can be set to whatever amount you want them to be; you can set the width to be a fixed one and the page to be zoomed in or out (`initial-scale`), but the well known, worldwide approach so far has been the following one:

```
<meta name="viewport" content="width=device-width, initial-scale=1.0">
```

And for good reason—since the trend of responsive or adaptive design, and the widespread acquisition of browser capable smartphones, people have started to browse the internet on their phones too, which are clearly different from the standard desktop and laptop screens.

The mobile browser's implementation initially attempted to show the whole page on the mobile screen (despite the different rules and settings involved in its creation), zooming it out automatically to horizontally fill the screen without scrolling bars.

Of course, on pages designed on the standard, fixed width of 960px, constraining them to a range that was one fourth of the original gave some irresponsible, unreadable, and non-navigable results.

,Even though this was years ago, it's hard to believe that this was the best design from mobile phone and browsers makers. I mean, even letting the page be zoomed at the actual size and letting users move around would have been a better, default solution.

Anyway, this situation caused a lot of rumors, crises in the World Wide Web; it also caused the adoption of and movement to the responsive and adaptive strategies.

One of the very first steps toward it was the preceding Meta declaration, which commanded mobile browsers to actually load the website on the entire width of the screen (at the initially designed dimensions) without zooming it out.

It's a declaration that every responsive website has and must have—without it, the mobile browser will take over and the visualization will be as shown in the previous screenshot and not like the one you thought of, even if it is coded responsively.

With the Meta addition the website start to behave correctly on mobile viewports.

Is that all? Is that everything we have to write about viewport, and how to scale things accordingly to it?

Certainly not! But, this introduction was verily needed — both, to explain what the actual viewport is and why some implementations tied to it were born.

CSS3 custom units

CSS3 brings to the table some new units that aren't really relative to the content they are applied to — they are tied to the actual viewport they're currently seen in.

A little bit like rems, if you want a quick comparison for a better understanding.

Named as viewport percentage lengths, they are as follows:

- vh: Viewport height
- vw: Viewport width
- vmin: Viewport minimum length
- vmax: Viewport maximum length

Viewport units are actually represented by percentages. 1vh means 1 percent of the visible area height.

Vmin instead is 1% of the smallest side, while Vmax is 1% of the largest side.

If you set measures with them, your layout can drastically change, for example, when the phone is held in portrait or landscape mode, so be careful.

It seems impractical, but it comes in handy in today's web design world.

Previously, such measures were handled by percentages, which are referred to the containing element, so you have to set measures for every item from the top to the bottom for them to apply. Otherwise, they would go unnoticed.

Now, think of styling a sidebar and a top bar and making them 25 percent and 100 percent of the visualized window respectively.

Doing it with vw is easy as it gets.

And, think about vertical centering (keep in mind that your window is 100vh), diving it to an equal bottom and top margin and giving it a height; well, it will stay in the vertical center no matter what.

Here is an example:

```
#try {
    width: 60vw;
    height: 60vh;
    margin: 20vh auto;
    background-color: #a4dd3c;
}
```

This will produce the following result:

Using them to overcome Bootstrap, and every other framework, for a full width result can't get easier.

If you want 4 columns, apply 25 vw to each one of them. If you want 8 columns, 12.5 vw, and so on.

While, it's easy to think of them for popups, bars, informative windows, and so on, one of the natural uses for these newborn units is indeed in typography. In fact, using these kinds of measures for your website typography makes sure the optimal line length of the paragraph is saved on all screen sizes.

Unfortunately there is no way of transforming previous pixels or ems measure into viewport percentage ones, they are too much different for us to achieve this. So the only real way is to build the measures by scratch, trying and adjusting them on the road.

Luckily, the scale method and previous values are still valid, so we can try to transfer them to the current typography (whereas if a number is too big, you can try adding a comma, for example, 20 rems can be 2 vw) so as to retain a perfect balance between type elements.

Unfortunately, with every new release and idea, support varies completely from browser to browser. Being supported since Chrome 20 and Safari 6, they are readable and render correctly, but they won't resize on window transformation. A complete refresh of the page in the new resolution is needed for typography to act properly.

The best solution is to use jQuery to force a refresh of the element itself while resizing. You can do this through something as small and simple as the following:

```
$(window).resize(function() {
    $("#object").css({ "font-size": "3vw" });
});
```

The preceding fuction is simply taking into account every window resize, forcing our defined viewport measure to be applied to the font-size property.

Another common solution is to play with something completely irrelevant to our object, such as z-index, again with simple jQuery:

```
refreshType = $("h1, h2, h3, p");

$(window).resize(function() {
  refreshType.css("z-index", 1);
});
```

This solution force the browser to refresh and apply the new z-index every time the window is resized, therefore refreshing the whole viewport area. Like the first, a beautiful solution too.

Luckily, this issue has been fixed for versions up to Chrome 34 and Safari 7, so it's up to you to integrate such solutions or not—it all depends on the backward compatibility of some specific features of your website.

Needless to say, Microsoft only supports them on its latest release, IE 10, while Firefox started with version 19, Android on its 4.4 release, and iOS since its sixth installment. But still, I don't know how many people resize the browser windows on their mobiles, so maybe back compatibility doesn't apply in that case.

Again, this approach isn't much different from what we previously encountered— such as ems, percentages, and rems.

After all, having just one percentage for type in the body tag that makes everything scale seems like a good solution. But still, from time to time, some manual adjustment may be needed, especially if you use big headings. With this new set of measures, adjustments won't be needed so much, not even a fixed starting point!

Still, we may encounter some cases where our type seems to get too big or too small. How can we act in those cases?

Here comes another CSS property (or function, which defines it better)!

Calc() is a native way for CSS to do simple math. It has four operators: + (add), − (subtract), * (multiply), and / (divide).

It's necessary to use a white space between the operators, otherwise the math formula won't work.

It certainly comes in handy when you need to do simple math on your CSS. And when is that ever needed?

Well, now is a time that it is.

To act and set a minimum and maximum font size, we need to know under which resolution they shrink or grow over those limitations — and this is something that involves a lot of trial and error, dragging windows, taking screenshots, and so on.

This is all boring and time consuming; as if bulletproof web developing wasn't taking enough time by itself.

Knowing the exact size we want our minimum to act in px, ems, or rems will suffice.

The following CSS formula will add one percent of the viewport size at every resolution/scaling, when the type falls within the set limit — whatever you want it to be:

```
body { font-size: calc(16px + 1vw); }
```

And, it's done!

Again, support still varies, so if you want to support, for example, IE8 and downward, you may declare a fallback measure before the calc rule (or before the vh ones too):

```
body { font-size: 1.2em;
   font-size: calc(0.85em + 1vw);
}
```

Getting a max is a little bit more complicated — we need to keep our max in mind and divide it by the result of our approximate similar value of viewport units divided by 100.

It goes something like this:

font-size / (viewport units / 100)

Using a 24px value and a similar 3vw value will mean that our font won't grow more than 24px on 800px sized viewports.

The way to apply this limit will be explored in the next chapter; we don't want to throw too much knowledge at you altogether; it will cause a mess.

It is better to proceed step by step.

Also, as of today, the min-font-size and max-font-size are slowly being introduced in the CSS specifications.

You can check the current state of requested implementation here `https://lists.w3.org/Archives/Public/www-style/2014Jul/0051.html`.

And this will surely turn out useful—but still, even with them, the preceding calculus of each of those values remains valid. It will only change where they need to be placed.

Let me thereby conclude this chapter by including a useful thing for you: a table of general vw measures at general breakpoint so that you can be more precise with your type proportions.

Viewport units					
Viewport / Size	1vw	2vw	3vw	4vw	5vw
400px	4px	8px	12px	16px	20px
500px	5px	10px	15px	20px	25px
600px	6px	12px	18px	24px	30px
700px	7px	14px	21px	28px	35px
800px	8px	16px	24px	32px	40px
900px	9px	18px	27px	36px	45px
1000px	10px	20px	30px	40px	50px

As a final tip, let me get back to the `calc()` function.

Sometimes when we code our way trough a website, we create a framework – or a multi-column structure – from scratch. Using `calc()` we can make our single columns handling a lot easier.

For example, the next function will show exactly that – dynamically calculating the width of a 7 columns structure trough simple divisions and multiplications.

```
.columnOne {
    width: calc(100% / 7);
}
.columnTwo{
    width: calc(100% / 7 * 2);
}
.columnThree {
    width: calc(100% / 7 * 3);
}
```

Doing so will allow your columns, rows, and divs, among others, to be responsive without any even measure that will leave undesired spaces, while also being auto-adjusting.

Sure, writing a complex structure like this takes time at first, but it will surely save you time and headaches in the long run.

Think about it, you won't regret it.

Summary

This was a short but notion fulfilling chapter.

We moved through the viewport notion on how to actually measure responsive objects with the viewport width and height measures.

These were also useful for the real, responsive vertical centring of your website sections.

As a final topic, you were introduced to and began using the calc() CSS property, which puts basic math under a useful web designer light.

In the next chapter, we will examine how pre-processors can handle some of our CSS faster, especially for typography. See you there!

6
Media Queries

While other technologies are searched, invented, and developed, there is something we can surely implement in today's world, with support going back to Firefox 3, Chrome 21 and so on: the CSS2-introduced `@media` tag.

Truly born as a media type, this tag allows for different stylesheets to be imported – or for different rules and behaviors to be described within the current one – when some condition happens. Their first usage was in fact built to provide the possibility to the user to print out the webpage in a friendly way.

No more dull colors, double sized paper or text so small as to be useless: the designer had the possibility to strip off everything from the website, leaving it barebones, allowing the user only to print a readable, hierarchical text with the vital images all following correct flow and alignments.

How to write them

The syntax is pretty straightforward – but the values are not, since some of them have been deprecated.

Starting with `@media` followed by the not/all expression, type and again not/all plus its features contained within ( ) – this rule actually has tons of applications.

Let's find all the types together:

- **All for types** means that the following CSS will be applied to every instance of every medium available
- **Aural** was use to style content for screen readers – with properties as beautiful as voice-volume, voice-balance, voice-rate, speech and so on...Now almost deprecated, with lots of its values moved to the speech media feature
- **Braille**, for (you guessed it) Braille tactile machines

- **Embossed** – this time to output content on Braille printers. The world is a beautiful place

- **Handheld** – crazy to think there once was such a term used in CSS, while as of today we opt for the simpler "mobile"

- **Print** – the majority of the work was usually put here, other values were ignored, unless you were in a specific business

- **Projection** – was used for screen projectors and presentation – never had that much use

- **Screen** – one of the pillars along with print. It is used to describe the content on every screen, from mobile to desktop.

- **Tty** – was used to translate the content for fixed grid screens and machines, like server terminals.

- **Tv** – won't sound new, but was used to translate the content on TV screens

The above describe and address the content for different kind of screens. All of them had some properties that could be addressed specifically, for the content to behave only on the meeting of those requirements, so let's see them too!

(They are named media features)

- **Aspect-ratio**: Describes the ratio between width and height of the viewport, to only address those with the specified measure (remember as earlier explained there's a difference between the screen size and the actual viewable area, which is the viewport).

- **Color**: Number of bits to obtain a specific color on the final screen (bit depth basically).

- **Color-index**: the number of colors the device is capable of showing.

- **Device-aspect-ratio**: And here it goes. Apart from the viewport, this value is specifically for the whole screen too.

- **Device-height** and **device-width** truly explain themselves.

- **Grid**: Aim of the device, if it's a terminal or a complete bitmap one.

- **Height** refers to the viewport height.

- **Max-aspect-ratio**: The maximum ratio between width and height of the desired, affected device.

- **Max-device-height, max-device-width, max-height, max-resolution** and their min variations need no explanations.

- **Monochrome** indicates the desired bits per color in a monochrome display, with min and max properties added.

- **Orientation** is really interesting. It addresses the behavior and display of your website, with values as portrait or landscape.**Overflow-block** targets content that exceeds the viewport width.

- **Resolution** targets the desired (of course) resolution of the device you tailored your content for.**Scan** means the scanning process of the device – since a text-to-speech machine uses a different process than a web browser, as a quick example.**Width** – well, this needs no explanation.

Media queries in the next CSS installment, **Media Queries Level 4**, added an option called Update Frequency, targeting the speed of change of the output for the desired machine.

Media queries for responsive design

After a mandatory introduction and overview, it's time to see what can be achieved using media queries today – and where they fit our process as responsive designers and developers.

Turns out they are the most powerful weapon inside our arsenal. Let's see them together.

Using the regular, standard compliant syntax, we can set up custom rules, called break-points, in our standard CSS without additional sheets.

When the content encounters those rules – the most common one being tied to the dimension of the screen – the layout/behavior of your website/element will change accordingly.

Let's start with something simple:

```
body{
   background-color: red;
}
@media only screen and (max-width: 500px) {  body {
     background-color: lightblue;  }}
```

This code – which can be written anywhere in your CSS – simply tells the browser to render the background in a light blue only when the screen is equal or less to 500px.

This is the situation when the page is first loaded:

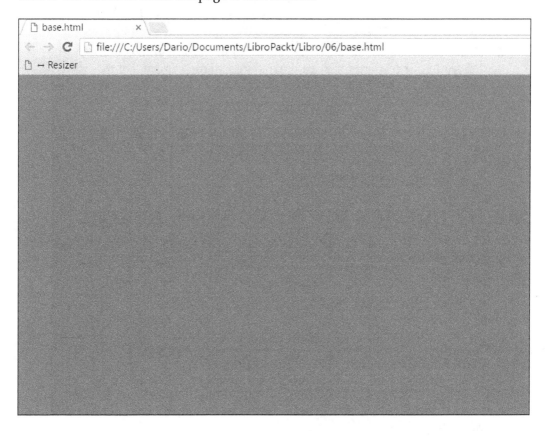

And this is what happens when the browser window gets resized under 500px:

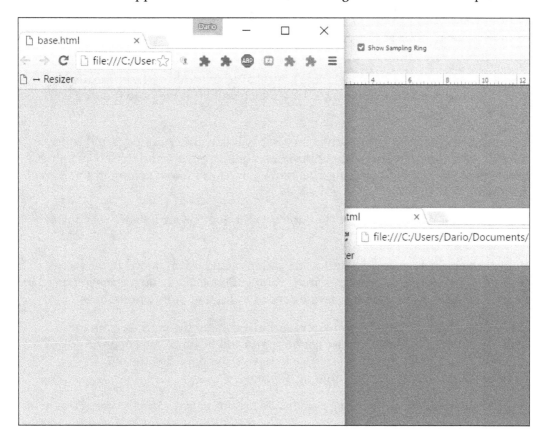

This can be useful for a variety of reasons, most of all, readability – for example changing background to a more contrasted one or completely scrapping the loading of a background image, reverting instead on colors when seeing your website on a mobile.

Of course, to set a median point you should just combine min and max-width like this:

```
@media screen and (min-width: 480px) and (max-width: 800px) { }
```

This will apply the code only to the resolutions between 480 and 800 pixels.

Can you already see the potential?

Imagine using them for moving and scaling around parts of our website, scaling fonts for mobile and so on. Well, that's exactly what we're going to do now.

First and foremost, we must apply the initial default (so feel free to change it as you see fit for your project) in the `<head>` of the html document:

```
<meta name="viewport" content="width=device-width, initial-
    scale=1">
```

The browser will make the page at the largest available width (the entire device width) with an initial zoom factor of 1:1 – which will keep the page the way you want it.

Without that crucial line, the mobile browser will take the entire page and squeeze it inside your device width without proper scaling, applying variable zoom values as it sees fit, like the old browsing on a mobile, when a lot of pinching to zoom was required.

Ok, time to get back to our CSS – but don't forget that line for all your responsive projects.

While breakpoints can be a multitude, they aren't standard anymore. In the recent past working with them meant designing for the iPhone, iPad and a Samsung flagship phone – so three/four resolutions were needed – and they were precise ones.

As of today, hundreds of different devices have entered the market, from the well-known ones, to their Chinese counterparts and beyond, each one with different screen and resolution sizes. So to have a standard like the old, beloved 480px or 960px means nothing anymore.

As of today, defining and writing responsive breakpoints means to work on content and layout first, scaling it later.

There are a variety of methods to do so – we settled on the Mobile First one, which focuses a lot on hierarchy and streamlining your websites as much as possible for it to be used on a smartphone, which is always a good idea. After all, a website is made to understand and experience, it is never just one or the other. Other UX enhancements may come – and be added – later.

Enough for the chit-chat, let's code!

We'll assume we're building a marketing website – so we lay down a bit of underlying structure:<div class="pagewrap">

```
<header id="header">

  <hgroup>
    <h1 id="site-logo">Demo</h1>
    <h2 id="site-description">Site Description</h2>
  </hgroup>

  <nav>
    <ul id="main-nav">
      <li><a href="#">Home</a></li>
    </ul>
  </nav>

  <form id="searchform">
    <input type="search">
  </form>

</header>

<div class="content">

  <article class="post">
    blog post
  </article>

</div>

<aside id="sidebar">

  <section class="widget">
    widget
  </section>

</aside>

<footer>
  footer
</footer>

</div>
```

This is a simple page with a sidebar and footer.

Remember that if you want to tackle earlier IEs than version 9 you can do so with this simple line of code – inserted in the head as always:

```
<!--[if lt IE 9]>
<script src=
    "http://html5shim.googlecode.com/svn/trunk/html5.js">
    </script>
<![endif]-->
```

It's a standard script that will make them recognize the new elements as `<footer>`, `<section>` and so on.

You can code it yourself, but why waste your precious time for such things – even more now that the death of supporting every IE prior to version 11 has been announced by Microsoft?

As we were saying – simple website, simple structure. It's time to define some basic CSS for it too:

```
pagewrap {
   max-width: 980px;
   margin: 0 auto;
}

#header {
   height: 160px;
}

.content {
   width: 80%;
   float: left;
   background-color: red;
}

#sidebar {
   width: 20%;
   float: right;
   background-color: silver;
}

footer {
   clear: both;
}
```

This is the simple page we have right now – yes, a marketing blog like we've seen before thousands of times. But this one is special: it is natively responsive and it's all ours.

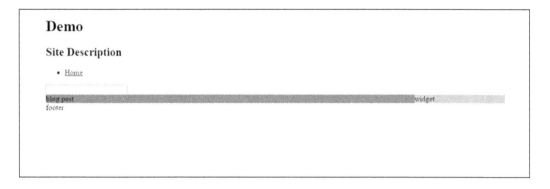

Now it's time to input our mystical CSS3 media queries for responsive design.

And again, if you want them to work on earlier IE versions, just add this to your masthead:

```
<!--[if lt IE 9]>
  <script src="http://css3-mediaqueries-
  js.googlecode.com/svn/trunk/css3-mediaqueries.js"></script>
<![endif]-->
```

So we'll just go and add these lines of code to our CSS:

```
@media screen and (max-width: 650px) {

  #header {
    height: auto;
  }

  #searchform {
    position: absolute;
    top: 5px;
    right: 0;
  }

  #main-nav {
    position: static;
  }

  #site-logo {
```

```
    margin: 15px 2% 5px 0;
    position: static;
  }

#site-description {
    margin: 0 0 15px;
    position: static;
  }

#content {
    width: auto;
    float: none;
    margin: 20px 0;
  }

#sidebar {
    width: 100%;
    float: none;
    margin: 0;
  }

}
```

Doing so will completely transform our structure as shown in the following screenshot:

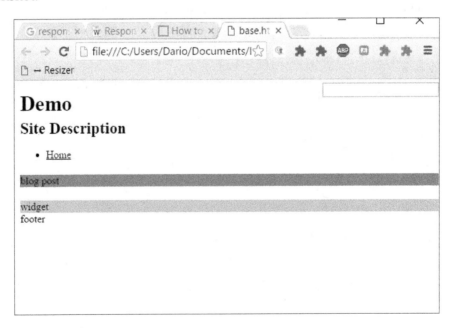

Simply add this line of code:

```
@media screen and (max-width: 650px) {
```

Then, add some properties, like positioning and change of width values. We have transformed our website behavior.

To make your images act responsive is simple. `Set max-width: 100%` and `height: auto` to make your images scale smoothly preserving their appearance and report.

And we could do more, like "erasing" the sidebar with its content from the mobile.

How? Just adding the value: `display: none;` with JavaScript – or your preferred language - to make it collapse (since the simple display solution will still have it taking up space, just being invisible) will work.

Of course there are bugs here and there in the implementation –the percentage rounding, for instance, which is not precise. But this can be resolved using `calc()`, that we've seen earlier.

Other known bugs that we feel obligated to mention are:

- The inclusion of the scrollbar in Firefox (which is not a bug, it's advised by the W3C itself – but it makes no sense. Basically, you'll have to consider around 15/20px to every absolute width measure since Firefox will consider the scrollbar as part of the user view area.

- The non-refresh of some display styles if the window gets resized. Corrected now, it was present in the early days of responsive web design,

- As it was thought, responsive is for native resolution – a website that is loaded once on one device with a fixed width, not for designers which literally passed the time altering their browser window, testing their and other developer's creations. The data download: since images aren't automatically resized and since content remains the same, mobile users download a lot of data that make the experience worse without being used. Avoid this so you can tackle the selectiveness of resources by Sass, Less, Ruby or any other language.

While all of the above is magical, you may think that this is a typography book and that I've actually lost my mind. Luckily not, since what stands true for the simple tutorial, stands true for typography: as content, it's tied to the container measure and behavior – and every rule and writing of the above applies in the same way to typography.

We are now in fact going to work with a little typography.

Addressing type with precision is a complex job that requires hours of work on any specific project – but to start, let me give you a couple of overhaul rules.

Limiting font scale below a specific threshold is really useful to limit the set of rules without many media queries.

Use:

```
html { font-size: 16px;   /* default below 600px */ }
@media (min-width: 600px){
  html {
    font-size: 3vw;
  }
}
```

Of course your desired breakpoint here is 600px. This will make sure that when the viewport is getting under your limit, your text appearance will be constant and fixed, without scaling or moving.

It can be useful to keep a constant character number, like the following image illustrate, whereas the red area keep its width despite the change in resolution

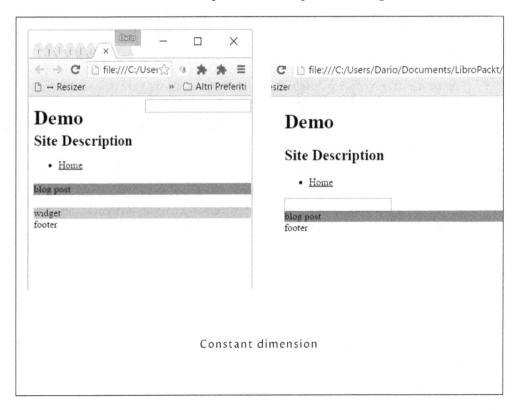

If you want to apply the above trick – but only when reaching a specified scaled type dimension, you can do so with a little math.

You first need to know which font size is the desired one, then you'll apply the following expression:

Font-size / (number of viewport units / 100)

For example, if we want our font up-scaling until 24px, we use the following expression

24 / (3 / 100) = 800px

So we'll set the code like this – always having the HTML `font-size` set at 16px:

```
@media (min-width: 800px){
   html {
      font-size: 1.5rem;   /*above 800px */
   }
}
```

Next time your website is seen at a resolution over 800px your text won't scale, keeping its appearance and character count per line.

After working all these years in the field, I have a table that I compiled with general values for readability that I'd like to gift to you.

Viewport.Units / Viewport.Size	1vw	2vw	3vw	4vw	5vw
500px	4px	8px	12px	16px	20px
500px	5px	10px	15px	20px	25px
600px	6px	12px	18px	24px	30px
700px	7px	14px	21px	28px	35px
800px	8px	16px	24px	32px	40px
900px	9px	18px	27px	36px	45px
1000px	10px	20px	30px	40px	50px

Using these values – both in font size with the above media queries expression will ensure an optimal legibility for your works.

Just remember that each project is different and that you can and should change the values according to your content

Summary

In this chapter we learnt what CSS3 media queries are, how to use them to define and apply specific rules to determined breakpoints in our CSS.

We learnt of their applicability to type and how to set a limit to our typography scaling, both with a deciding viewport width – or a desired type size.

And lastly but not least, I gifted you with a useful table describing viewport sizes in combination with desired point sizes for optimal readability

In the next chapter we are going to explore a mix of SASS with typography, so tighten your belt.

7
Sass and Typography

Welcome back!

In the previous chapters we learnt a lot about responsive design, what it is and how to apply it through modern HTML and CSS properties, like the Media Queries seen in the latest chapter (which I'm sure you loved).

Within this chapter, we will learn how to implement some of those properties and knowledge with one of the CSS preprocessors, Sass.

CSS pre-processors and Sass

As always, before proceeding with elbows deep in code we must learn and become acquainted with some theory.

You may want to start and code the moment you lay your eyes on the page, but doing so will produce a coder blind to its surroundings – and that's not what I want or what the world needs.

A CSS preprocessor allows you to write CSS files in a modular way. It will be easier for you to write your code and change it in the future since you'll basically write less rules directly, through the use of concepts as variables, functions, mixins, and so on. You'll basically program your CSS, more than write it directly on the page.

It also makes maintaining complex systems easier. There are a lot of these tools available, the most famous ones being Sass and LESS.

Sass and LESS: A comparison

They run on two different languages: Sass is Ruby based while LESS is a JavaScript library, so even their installation is different.

[Ruby is an object-oriented programming language focused on simplicity of learning and writing. It was invented in mid-1990 by Yukihiro Matsumoto]

For this reason, LESS can be installed by simply linking the library in your document, while Sass requires Ruby installed on the machine and then to be called itself through the command line.

They both have variables which are constant CSS rules – such as font-type or a colors definition. It means that you can define color as a variable and simply call them through your entire document with one simple word – or CSS style and attributes, without having to remember different hex codes every time. Pretty neat, huh?

Anyway the difference here is minimal: Sass defines variables with the $ sign, while LESS uses @.

Nesting is also neat: using it you won't have to write many selectors repeatedly. I know you don't understand me still, so let me show you what I mean by nesting, since it's easier when seen than when heard:

```
nav {
    margin: 50px auto 0;
    width: 788px;
    height: 45px;
    ul {
        padding: 0;
        margin: 0;
    }
border: {
    style: solid;
    left: {
      width: 4px;
      color: #333333;
    }
    right: {
      width: 2px;
      color: #000000;
    }
  }
}
```

See what I mean? The border property is nested/taken into the nav variable – and additional border properties that we all know as left and right are nested inside the border.

Take into account that this is only possible through Sass and not through LESS – with LESS left and right should be defined outside the border definition.

When compiled it will generate a classic CSS file with the following rules:

```
nav {
  margin: 50px auto 0;
  width: 788px;
  height: 45px;
  border-style: solid;
  border-left-width: 4px;
  border-left-color: #333333;
  border-right-width: 2px;
  border-right-color: #000000;
}
nav ul {
  padding: 0;
  margin: 0;
}
```

See the potential? It was easier to read, to write, and to remember – while still giving birth to the same old CSS we and the browsers know. In the future, if you want to update or change something you'll do it just once, and compile and upload the new CSS file – without having to search and change multiple variables.

Sounds awesome? That's because it is!

Mixins in both tools are used to apply one rule to another, speeding up the writing.

Their application vary a bit from Sass to LESS, let's see how with the following example:

In Sass mixin are declared like the following:

```
@mixin border-radius ($values) {
    border-radius: $values;
}
nav {
    @include border-radius(10px);
    margin: 50px auto 0;
    width: 788px;
    height: 45px;
}
```

In LESS mixin are declared like:

```
.border(@radius) {
    border-radius: @radius;
}
nav {
    margin: 50px auto 0;
    width: 788px;
    height: 45px;
    .border(10px);
}
```

This will apply the 10px border every time the border is called.

Sass takes it a little bit further, because while copying the whole properties is useful – just copying one word is even more.

With the @extend syntax, you can take a defined rule and apply it without any additional rewriting, like the following example:

```
.circle {
    border: 1px solid #ccc;
    border-radius: 50px;
    overflow: hidden;
}
.avatar {
    @extend .circle;
}
```

When compiled, the above will result in strict CSS:

```
.circle, .avatar {
  border: 1px solid #ccc;
  border-radius: 50px;
  overflow: hidden;
}
```

See? Same properties without additional fuss.

Also, do you remember the calc() property I explained a couple of chapters ago?

Sass and LESS can do it without strict syntax, only terms.

The following code will return the result (and apply it in the CSS) between the comment tags:

```
$margin: 20%;
div {
    margin: $margin - 10%; /* 10% */
}
```

Keep in mind that while LESS will erroneously perform such basic operations, even between different indicators, Sass will more rightfully return an error like the following:

```
$margin: 10px;
div {
    margin: $margin - 10%; /* Syntax error:
    Incompatible
        units: '%' and 'px' */
}
```

For all the above reasons we choose to standardize this book and chapter to the Sass preprocessor and not LESS, as it will allow us to do more things in less (pun intended) time.

Installing Sass

As said, installing Sass is not as straightforward as LESS – you need to install Ruby first (which on a Mac is preinstalled, on a Windows machine, unfortunately not).

Then you need to install Sass through the command line.

Luckily there are apps available to do it through a GUI. As always, some of them are paid, some of them free of cost.

The full list is available on the Sass website at: http://sass-lang.com/install

The full list in no particular order:

- CodeKit
- Compass.app (sadly abandoned)
- Ghostlab
- Hammer
- Koala
- LiveReload

- Prepros
- Scout

For this book we're going to use Koala, which is free and features a lovely, cute animal. What do you want more?

You can download the installer here: `http://koala-app.com/`:

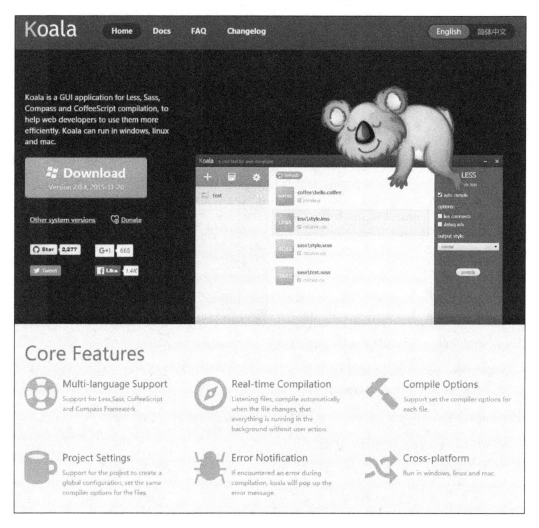

After installing it you can run it and see the principal window where you can define or add an already defined project (read it as website).

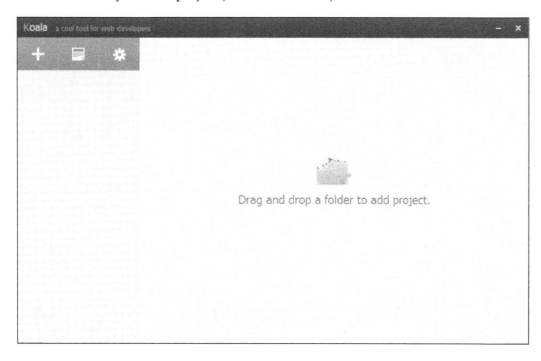

When working with Koala keep in mind you will be writing CSS as Sass, not direct CSS – and thus a .scss extension file.

To obtain the browser-readable, classic CSS, the file needs to be compiled/read as magically processed by eucalyptus-eating, cute animals.

Luckily, Koala runs the compilation in the background – and while you can set some compilation rules, the default is more than good for us and our purpose.

In fact, Koala will automatically compile in the background every time a change is being made – and save the new file in the original path.

So let's start a small tutorial project. Click on the plus **+** icon in the upper-left and select your folder. I named it Typography.

Of course, our folder is empty and we must create a Sass file for it to compile: we'll do so in our preferred code editing software (in my case Adobe Dreamweaver).

Yes, you'll work as you always do with the software you always use – but Koala, this time, will run in the background and take the file you're working on and transform it to CSS in real time.

Awesome, isn't it?

So open your preferred code editor, create a new file and save it as .sass or .scss (They are both good and just for development, you won't need to link them to your HTML page).

.sass is a concise version of Sass syntax, where brackets and semicolons are substituted by indentations.

.scss is a more recent format, derivative of CSS3 syntax that relies more on brackets and semicolons.

You can also take an existing CSS file and rename its extension to .sass or .scss (even if I advise against it, since your previous code won't adhere to the Sass rules from the beginning).

If you created it in our **Tutorial** folder, Koala should now have this interface:

This indicates that it recognizes our file. Click on it and the sidebar will appear. Click on **Auto Compile**, output as nested, and you're good to go!

It will automatically create our (initially empty) CSS file!

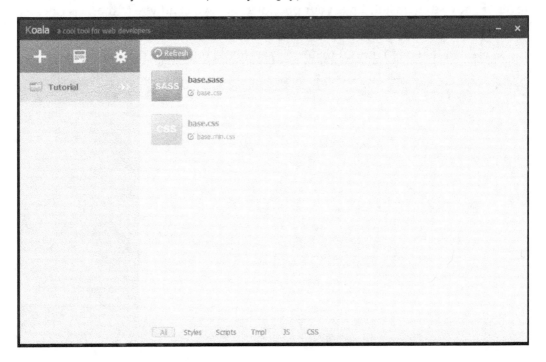

Just keep in mind we'll be working on the Sass file and that for each change we produce, the CSS file will be automatically generated – and you're good to go!

Your small Sass tutorial

This is a book about typography – and not Sass – but let's make a couple of functions to warm you up with it, in case it's your first encounter.

Let's start by defining a base color for a website – so in the .sass file, write this:

```
$blue: #08B
$fontBase: 16px


h1 {
  color: $blue;
}
p {
  color: darken($blue, 10%);
}
```

With this simple code we declared our level 1 headings to be blue (not the browser blue, our blue) and we asked it to be applied with a 10% darker tone to our paragraphs.

Yes, darken and lighten are basic, useful Sass functions. As saturate and desaturate, adjust-hue, tint, and shade.

As we learned earlier, doing basic operations through the same variables is possible.

What is unbelievably wonderful is the fact that you can add and subtract hex values.

Let's see what this little snippet will give us:

```
$blue: #08B;
$fontBase: 24px;

h1 {
  color: $blue;
}
p {
  color: $blue - #101;
  font-size: $fontBase;
}
```

When applied to this simple HTML document:

```
<!doctype html>
<html>
  <head>
    <meta charset="utf-8">
    <title>Simple tutorial</title>
    <link href="base.css" rel="stylesheet" type="text/css">
  </head>

  <body>
    <h1>I'm a simple H1 Heading</h1>
    <p>I'm a simple text, can you spot the color difference?</p>
  </body>
</html>
```

This is how our browser will render it:

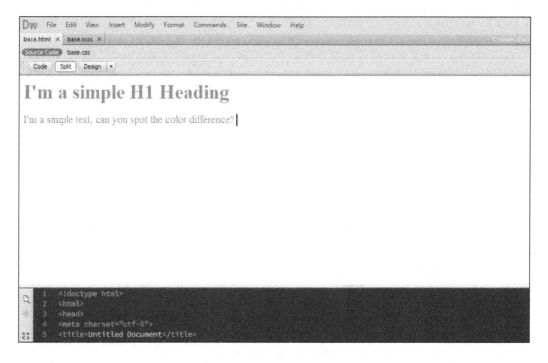

Need I say more?

More Sass properties

Nestings, as said, are the basics of writing SASS – and a useful, visual guide for your eye and document. See the following:

```
nav {
  ul {
    margin: 0;
    padding: 0;
    list-style: none;
  }

  li { display: inline-block; }

  a {
    display: block;
    padding: 1%;
  }
}
```

This will simply become this:

```
nav ul {
   margin: 0;
   padding: 0;
   list-style: none;
}

nav li {
   display: inline-block;
}

nav a {
   display: block;
   padding: 1%;
}
```

Partials are small Sass files that will not generate a CSS file – but that can be useful to compartmentalize your development so that you'll find changes in your website sections in an easier way.

To obtain a partial inside your project, just add an underscore in front of the name file.

So you'll have this:

`BigSassFile.scss`

`_partialSassFile.scss`

You'll then use your partial with the `import` property.

It won't generate additional HTTP requests as its CSS counterpart would, but will generate one single CSS file with the additional properties.

If your partial contains some code, running an import in your big file will look like this:

```
@import 'partialSassFile'
```

The underscore or file extension won't be needed – and the properties contained in the partial file will be brought and written directly in your main CSS.

Mixins can be basically seen as containers that are used to group and store various declarations (including variables themselves).

You'll declare them starting with an @ - and call them through `@include`. Useful for code that is repeated in your CSS.

See the following:

```
@mixin border-radius($radius) {
  -webkit-border-radius: $radius;
    -moz-border-radius: $radius;
     -ms-border-radius: $radius;
         border-radius: $radius;
}


.box { @include border-radius(10px); }
```

This will transform into the following:

```
.box {
  -webkit-border-radius: 10px;
  -moz-border-radius: 10px;
  -ms-border-radius: 10px;
  border-radius: 10px;
}
```

The extend property is one of the most useful properties in Sass. It will help you share properties between one selector and another without having to write everything again.

See the following:

```
.message {
  border: 1px solid #ccc;
  padding: 10px;
  color: #333;
}

.success {
  @extend .message;
  border-color: green;
}

.error {
  @extend .message;
  border-color: red;
}

.warning {
  @extend .message;
  border-color: yellow;
}
```

This will transform into this simple, clean CSS:

```
.message, .success, .error, .warning {
  border: 1px solid #cccccc;
  padding: 10px;
  color: #333;
}

.success {
  border-color: green;
}

.error {
  border-color: red;
}

.warning {
  border-color: yellow;
}
```

Lovely, isn't it?

And as said it supports **operators** for simple math operations such as + - / * and %. You'll just have to input them in the object properties.

Sass for responsive typography

Now that we have run a little background check on Sass, it's time to see how useful it can be when working with responsive web design and typography.

As we saw with our last chapter, where we made the additional knowledge of breaking points with media queries, keeping track of vertical rhythm and size values can become a hard and long, tedious job.

But we can use Sass maps for the job. Sass maps? What are they?

Glad you asked. Introduced in Sass 3.3 is a collection of values which can be called through one single call to make our development easier and faster.

We'll write the following map with our breakpoints:

```
$p-font: (
  null   : 15px,
  480px  : 16px,
  640px  : 17px,
  1024px: 19px
);
```

The null value is hereby needed because without the definition of every variable, when compiled the code will give us errors – which are portrayed here as shown by Koala:

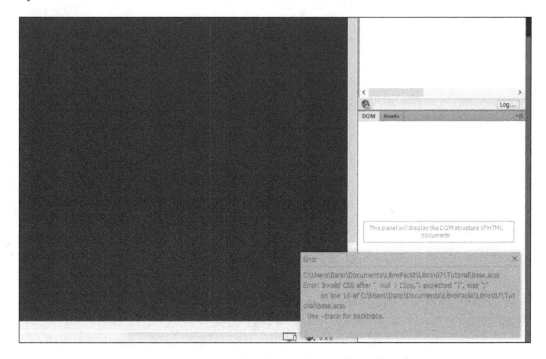

With the null value, which is a basic Sass one, we'll not have to define an additional breakpoint until, or if, needed – and they won't be compiled into our CSS (think of null as a zero render value for CSS) which will make it cleaner and weigh less.

In this case, having it as the base breakpoint won't throw any additional values, having the default point size defined through the entire site.

OK, so let's continue with our practical, vertical rhythm Sass example:

```scss
@mixin font-size($fs-map) {
  @each $fs-breakpoint, $fs-font-size in $fs-map {
    @if $fs-breakpoint == null {
      font-size: $fs-font-size;
    }
    @else {
      @media screen and (min-width: $fs-breakpoint) {
        font-size: $fs-font-size;
      }
    }
  }
}
```

It's time for a basic mixin which prints the breakpoints as standard CSS – and time to apply mixin to define our basic p element:

```
p {
  @include font-size($p-font);
}
```

Everything above will clearly result in the following CSS:

```
p {
  font-size: 15px; }
  @media screen and (min-width: 480px) {
    p {
      font-size: 16px; } }
  @media screen and (min-width: 640px) {
    p {
      font-size: 17px; } }
  @media screen and (min-width: 1024px) {
    p {
      font-size: 19px; } }
```

That's it!

Managing font size and breakpoints becomes a lot easier: all you have to do is create a map for every additional element you want defined, like first level headings for example:

```
$h1-font: (
  null   : 28px
  480px  : 31px,
  640px  : 33px,
  1024px : 36px
);

h1 {
  @include font-size($h1-font);
}
```

This will result in the following CSS:

```
h1 {
  font-size: 28px; }
  @media screen and (min-width: 480px) {
    h1 {
      font-size: 31px; } }
  @media screen and (min-width: 640px) {
```

```
    h1 {
      font-size: 33px; } }
  @media screen and (min-width: 1024px) {
    h1 {
      font-size: 36px; } }
```

In case we want our Map to be included into multiple variables we just declare them the usual way, like the following example:

```
p, ul, ol {
  @include font-size($p-font);
}
```

Too many breakpoints

Yes, this solution, while making writing and maintaining custom, responsive typography a lot easier, also gave birth to a fragmentation of CSS writing with too many breakpoint repetitions.

Is there a solution? I bet you already guessed it: Sass maps.

We'll define a map for our breakpoints:

```
$breakpoints: (
  small : 480px,
  medium: 640px,
  large : 1024px
);

$p-font: (
  null   : 15px,
  small  : 16px,
  medium: 17px,
  large : 19px
);

$h1-font: (
  null   : 28px,
  small  : 31px,
  medium: 33px,
  large : 36px
);
```

It's now time to modify our little mixin a bit, so that when it travels through the font map it will act accordingly to our breakpoint names to get their values:

```
@mixin font ($fs-map, $fs-breakpoints: $breakpoints) {
  @each $fs-breakpoint, $fs-font in $fs-map {
    @if $fs-breakpoint == null {
      font-size: $fs-font;
    }
    @else {
      @if map-has-key($fs-breakpoints, $fs-breakpoint) {
        $fs-breakpoint: map-get($fs-breakpoints, $fs-breakpoint);
      }
      @media screen and (min-width: $fs-breakpoint) {
        font-size: $fs-font;
      }
    }
  }
}
```

The Sass `map-has-key` is a standard Sass function that checks if a map has a specified value, in this case our breakpoints; the `map-get` is a standard function that gets called if the `map-has-key` has found values, in fact extracting them.

All of the above will result in our CSS:

```
p { font-size: 15px; }

@media screen and (min-width: 480px) {
  p { font-size: 16px; }
}
@media screen and (min-width: 700px) {
  p { font-size: 17px; }
}
@media screen and (min-width: 900px) {
  p { font-size: 18px; }
}
@media screen and (min-width: 1024px) {
  p { font-size: 19px; }
}
@media screen and (min-width: 1440px) {
  p { font-size: 20px; }
```

Adding line-height

We know vertical rhythm relies heavily on line-height as well. To add it to our functions we'll simply add it as a numerical value to our P and H1 elements and we're good to go:

```
$p-font: (
  null   : (15px, 1.3),
  small : 16px,
  medium: (17px, 1.4),
  large : (19px, 1.45),
);
```

We'll then need to modify the mixin to include line-height when generating the CSS:

```
@mixin font ($fs-map, $fs-breakpoints: $breakpoints) {
  @each $fs-breakpoint, $fs-font in $fs-map {
    @if $fs-breakpoint == null {
      @include make-font-size($fs-font);
    }
    @else {
      @if map-has-key($fs-breakpoints, $fs-breakpoint) {
        $fs-breakpoint: map-get($fs-breakpoints, $fs-breakpoint);
      }
      @media screen and (min-width: $fs-breakpoint) {
        @include make-font-size($fs-font);
      }
    }
  }
}
@mixin make-font-size($fs-font) {
  @if type-of($fs-font) == "list" {
    font-size: nth($fs-font, 1);
    @if (length($fs-font) > 1) {
      line-height: nth($fs-font, 2);
    }
  }
  @else {
    font-size: $fs-font;
  }
}
```

The mixin now checks the value of font map to see whether it is a list, instead of only one size (if the values are majors of 1) and in this case get and insert the correct values by nth index, assuming the first is size and second line-length, generating the following CSS:

```
p {
  font-size: 15px;
  line-height: 1.3; }
  @media screen and (min-width: 480px) {
    p {
      font-size: 16px; } }
  @media screen and (min-width: 700px) {
    p {
      font-size: 17px;
      line-height: 1.4; } }
  @media screen and (min-width: 1024px) {
    p {
      font-size: 19px;
      line-height: 1.45; } }
```

This solution is easy to implement and enlarge, adding margins, weights and so on.

We just have to modify the `make-font-size` mixin and the nth index to achieve our result.

Just keep coherent writing and you'll be good to go.

Of course instead of pixels you can use viewport units, percentages and whatever you need them to be.

Summary

In this long but useful chapter we learnt what preprocessors are, the differences between the two most popular ones – and we learned how to use Sass, through its:

- Variables
- Partials
- Import function
- Math operators
- Lighten and darken properties
- Maps

And we used Sass to configure our breakpoints and text elements through them, making it easier to write and maintain your CSS.

In the next chapters we will do a recap of what we learnt 'til now – and we'll also explore the future of type on the web.

I bet you had a ton of fun!

8
Three Step Responsive

Hi again dear reader, glad to see you made it this far!

This chapter will be a wrap-it-up where we'll cover all the precedent notions and make ourselves a nifty looking and acting website.

We'll decide which technologies are best for the current state of the web and which aren't; it's time to test our knowledge for the real world, so buckle up and let's go!

It actually takes more than three steps

To make a responsive, working website – as it's easy to imagine, and as we learned through the previous chapters – the core of its functionalities are indeed hosted in three sections:

- Meta tag, tells the browser to actually render the website the way you want it `<meta name="viewport" content="width=device-width, initial-scale=1.0">`

- The actual layout, ordered coding, and tags will make the job easier. Using a preprocessor like LESS or Sass actually helps a lot

- CSS3 Media Queries, since they are the most supported way to tell a browser how to react to different breaking points

So through this chapter we'll take everything from the above, to anything said in the past, to build our truly responsive website in one page – plus other bits to spice it up in the use of Sass and responsive design – and make you ready for all the outstanding future trials you'll encounter.

It will be a journey full of code, so make up your mind, gather some Marathon bars and a whole lot of coffee and follow our lead.

A Sass powered one page website

Let's start with our first, chapter-length project: imagine you are a designer, let's make a responsive one page website with Sass, showcasing your works.

First we'll create our project folder – and HTML page, of course naming it as standard, `index.html` – and the Sass file for our CSS, `style.scss`.

The following image show the structure of our project in its early minutes, using Koala and any of the developing software you use for your HTML and CSS (in this case Adobe Dreamweaver):

Let's start with our first step in responsive design, the meta tag in our `index.html` document:

```
<!DOCTYPE html>
<html>
  <head>
    <title>My Portfolio</title>
    <meta name="viewport" content="width=device-width,
    initial-scale=1">
    <!--[if IE]>
      <script src=
      "http://html5shiv.googlecode.com/svn/trunk/html5.js">
      </script>
    <![endif]-->
  </head>
  <body>
  </body>
</html>
```

Of course, we also added the htmlify scripts for HTML5 tags, in case we're addressing older browsers that don't support them.

We'll then start by injecting a little color on our page through future typography, making it dark gray – and while it looks like we're writing standard CSS, as we learned in our last chapter, we're actually writing Sass in our `.scss` document:

```
body {
    color: #333;
}
```

Saving it will make Koala autocompile our standard CSS document, which we can now link in our project.

Nothing strange or new here, we'll just link the auto-generated CSS as it was a normal one:

```
<link href="style.css" rel="stylesheet" type="text/css">
```

And this is how our working area in Koala appears:

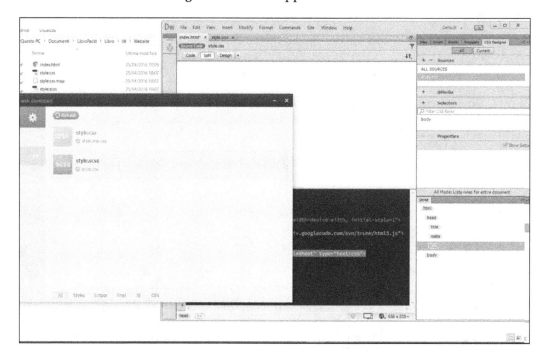

For our typography needs, we're going to use Google Web Fonts – as we already discussed, they are beautiful and free – so why not use them for our tutorial?

I'm going to use PT Serif for my titles, so I'm firstly going to add it to my collection:

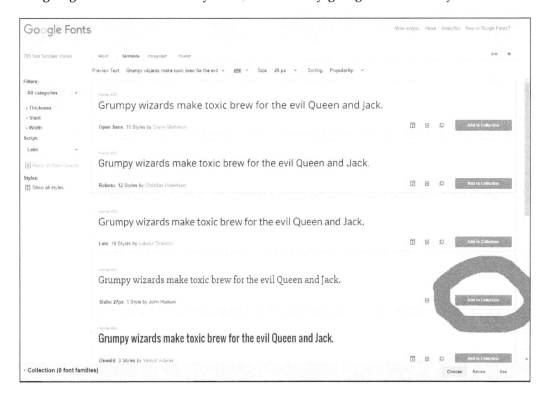

Then I'm going to press **Use** right below it – and since it only has one style, I'm just going to copy-paste the selected code in my HTML head section:

```
<link href='https://fonts.googleapis.com/css?family=PT+Serif:400,400it
alic' rel='stylesheet' type='text/css'>
```

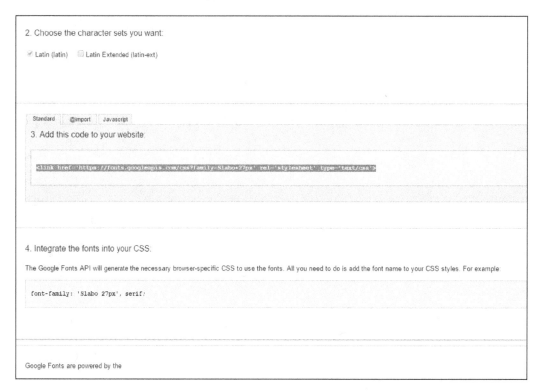

Then I need to call it inside our Sass document through a simple name property:

```
h1 {
    font-family: "PT Serif", Georgia, serif;
}
```

Anyway, onto the next step. Creating the header for our page.

As a one-page portfolio, we're making our header part of our presentation, with an image/avatar of ourselves and a brief description.

I created the avatar image to be 200x200px, but we'll use it at 100x100px, addressing our retina monitors as well.

I created an `images` folder in our project folder, so feel free to customize that bit and any that follow in any way you feel is better for your project.

Anyway, the following code needs to be typed inside our body, in our HTML document:

```
<header class="header">
    <img src="images/profile.jpg" id="avatar" />
    <h1>Hello, I'm Dario Calonaci. <br />I'm a designer
        specialized into Typography.</h1>
</header>
```

And this into our Sass document:

```
#avatar {
    width: 100px;
    height: 100px;
}
```

Your website will now appear like this:

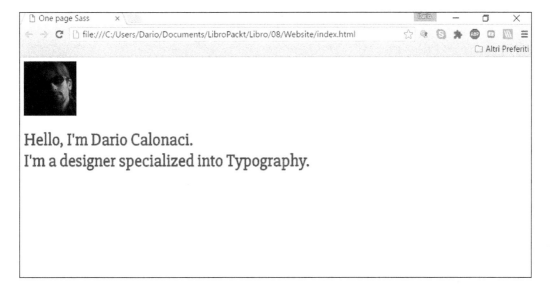

It's time to style a little of our page, including our basic typography, so let's add the following bits of code into our existing material inside our Sass document:

```
// Basic Page Styles
body {
    text-align: center;
    font: 1em/1.5 Verdana, sans-serif;
}

a {
```

```
        text-decoration: none;
    }

    img {
        max-width: 100%;
        height: auto;
    }
```

You shall notice that in Sass it's cool to comment single lines as `//`, while in standard CSS it would have been better to use the `/**/` formula.

Now our whole content will be centered.

Time to style our level 1 headings, since we'll be using them in each and every section of our website, so let's type this:

```
h1 {
    font-family: "PT Serif", Georgia, serif;
    font-size: 2.25em;
    padding: 0 1em;
}
```

 Notice we are working on ems with the very basic notion of 1em, since it's the most compatible way to work with typography on the web.

We'll style our header text, nesting our titles to use the italics of the web font we choose. Notice, as explained in the last chapter, that nesting in Sass is an advanced, and also required, way of working toward better written, standard-compliant CSS, the fast way.

In fact, see the following Sass code:

```
header {
    padding: 10em 0 14em;

    h1 {
        font-style: italic;
    }
}
```

When compiled, this will generate the following, standard-compliant CSS:

```
header {
  padding: 10em 0 14em; }
  header h1 {
    font-style: italic; }
```

Time to style our profile image with Sass too:

```
#avatar {
box-shadow: 0 0 0px 3px #fff, 0 0 0 4px #ccc, 0 4px 6px #333;
    border-radius: 50%;
}
```

Adding the above two lines to our image will simply add more style – and will crop it in a circle shape, since the border radius is half our original display size.

This is what we have thus far:

We're now going to populate our page with our works – what better way than to add them manually and update them each and every time?

We're going to populate the page with our Dribbble profile that works in a horizontal carousel and use HTML5 and CSS3 to add touch interactivity,

Let's start with the simple HTML markup:

```
<section class="dribbble">
    <h1 class="dribbble">Latest works</h1>

    <div class="carousel">
        <div class="shots-container">
            <ul class="shots"></ul>
        </div>

    </div>

    <p>& larr; scroll to view &rarr;</p>
</section>
```

Taking the content from Dribbble and injecting into our page is simple, using JavaScript and the Dribbble API.

So we are going to create a JavaScript file to communicate with the Dribbble API – and a call to jQuery in remote on our page.

Add the following two lines before our closing `</body>` tag:

```
<script src="http://ajax.googleapis.com/ajax/libs/jquery/1.8.3/jquery.
min.js"></script>
<script src="javascripts/dribbble.js"></script>
```

Of course, according to the above code, we placed our JS files in a folder called `javascripts`.

So let's move to our `Dribbble.js` file.

We're declaring two variables that we'll use to intake and inject the shots into:

```
var dribbbleUsername = 'dcalonaci';

// Variable to hold the HTML we'll generate
var html = '';
```

`dribbbleUsername` is simply the name you're going to take the shots from – and the HTML variable is where we're going to inject them.

Now we are going to request from Dribbble API something with the following code:

```
$.getJSON("http://api.dribbble.com/players/"+ dribbbleUsername +"/
shots?callback=?", function(data) {
    // Use the results here
});
```

Dribbble API will recognize our call, since the URL is the player's variable – and will understand we want the shots from a username-specified user. So it will inject JSON in the data function callback.

Knowing the Dribbble API and the JSON it just returned, we are going to address just three variables that we need.

- image_url for the shot image
- title for the shot name
- url for the shot URL

And for the .shots section we are going to run a loop with the defined variables above, adding them to our next defined .shots section.

```
var numberOfShots = 12;

for (i=0; i<numberOfShots; i++) {
    html += '<li>';
    html += '<a href="'+ data.shots[i].url +'">';
    html += '<img src="' + data.shots[i].image_url + '" alt="'+
    data.shots[i].title +'" />';
    html += '</a>';
    html += '</li>';
}


$('.shots').html(html);
```

We'll define a variable numberOfShots with our wanted numbers and inserting the simple HTML list markup to obtain something like this:

```
<li>
    <a href="url">
        <img src="image_url" alt="title" />
    </a>
</li>
```

Simple, isn't it?

Another solution using JRibbble

Since Dribbble recently updated their API, the above might not work sometimes – I decided to leave it in the book as a working example – and, since it's a way for you to learn how to retrieve JSON from an API, a useful lesson.

But it's now time to implement our shots using an already existing JS library, called JRibbble. You can find it on http://lab.tylergaw.com/jribbble/.

So everything right now remains unchanged, we are just going to substitute the code above our closing body tag from the following:

```
<script src="http://ajax.googleapis.com/ajax/libs/jquery/1.8.3/jquery.
min.js"></script>
<script src="dribbble.js"></script>
```

We will change it to:

```
<script src="http://ajax.googleapis.com/ajax/libs/jquery/1.8.3/jquery.
min.js"></script>
<script src="jribbble.min.js"></script>
```

Simple as that. To make JRibbble work – due to the recent changes in the Dribbble API – we'll need to register an application on the Dribbble website, at the following URL:

```
https://dribbble.com/account/applications
```

This will help us to gain an access token for each profile. Yes, each of you reading should register an app.

I will post the code for my profile here – but it will only work with mine.

After adding the above scripts – we'll give our access token to JRibbble, with the following script:

```
<script>
$.jribbble.setToken('020db302752672c7240f035d207cc6edb6082eb001ad350d5
114d0a1aa2c0652');

$.jribbble.users('dcalonaci').shots({per_page: 12}).
then(function(shots) {
  var html = [];

  shots.forEach(function(shot) {
    html.push('<li class="shots--shot">');
    html.push('<a href="' + shot.html_url + '" target="_blank">');
    html.push('<img src="' + shot.images.normal + '">');
    html.push('</a></li>');
  });

  $('.shots').html(html.join(''));
});
  </script>
```

The setToken code will be taken from the created app – while the defined user, in this case dcalonaci, will tell the app what shots are needed.

With the latest code – and the JRibbble application, our page will now look like this:

Hello, I'm Dario Calonaci.
I'm a designer specialized into Typography.

Latest works

Sass stylizing our carousel

It's time to apply some visual style to our carousel, with our lovely Sass.

Writing the following code in our `Style.scss` file:

```
.carousel {
    position: relative;
}

.shots-container {
    width: 100%;
    overflow-x: scroll;
    -webkit-overflow-scrolling: touch;
    position: relative;
    padding: 1em 0;
}
```

We do give our shots container horizontal direction and hidden scroll through touch interaction where supported, in a much smoother fashion than anything JavaScript related.

We now need to line the shots horizontally, so it's time to work on our unordered list:

```
.shots {
    overflow: hidden;
    margin: 0;
    padding: 0 2%;
    /*
     * Shot width = 400px + 20px margin + 20px padding + 2px border
     * 442 * 6 (# of shots)
     */
    width: 2652px;
    min-height: 300px;

    @media screen and (max-width: 450px) {
        /*
         * Shot width = 300px + 20px margin + 20px padding + 2px
border
         * 342 * 6 (# of shots)
         */
        width: 2052px; /* 340 * 10 */
        min-height: 250px;
    }

    li {
        float: left;
        width: 400px;
        height: 300px;
        margin: 0 10px;
        padding: 10px;
        background: #fff 100px 50% no-repeat;
        border: 1px solid #ddd;
        border-radius(3px);

        @media screen and (max-width: 450px) {
            width: 300px;
            height: 225px;
        }
    }
}
```

All of the above Sass code will do the following:

We give the unordered list `.shots` – that JRibbble injected with our desired number of shots, in this case 12 – a fixed width, that, based on the above commented calculations, will display us six shots for columns. The overlapping content will be scrollable natively.

We also implemented a work in progress breakpoint, which we almost always get with a lot of trial and error, since there isn't really a standard resolution anymore.

Here is how the website will now appear:

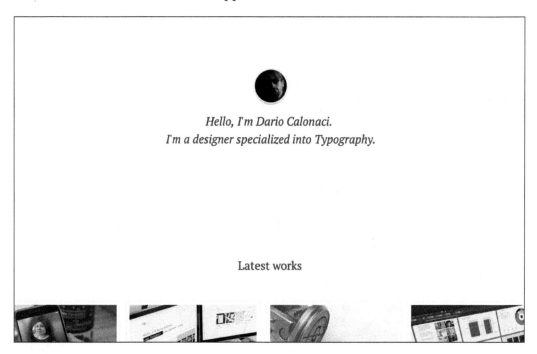

It's now time to add a little footer to our one-page website.

We'll write a little markup in our HTML document:

```
<footer>
    <h1>Find Me on the Web</h1>
    <p>You can contact or follow me via any of these services:</p>
    <ul class="social">
        <li><a href="#">Facebook</a></li>
        <li><a href="#">Twitter</a></li>
        <li><a href="#">Behance</a></li>
```

```
        <li><a href="#">Dribbble</a></li>
    </ul>
</footer>
```

It's time for some basic styling:

```
footer {
    p {
        color: #777;
        padding: 0 1em;
    }
}

header,
footer {
    background: #f7f7f7;
}

footer {
    padding: 3em 0 6em;
}

.dribbble {
    padding: 1em 0 1em;

    h1 {
        color: #ea4c89;
    }

    > p {
        font-size: .85em;
        color: #aaa;
    }
}
```

This will result in something like this:

Now we want to add icons to our simple links in the future – and since we want them to be responsive and resolution independent, we're going to use an icon font.

For this to work we are going to generate our own icon font through the great service that is at: `https://icomoon.io/app/`.

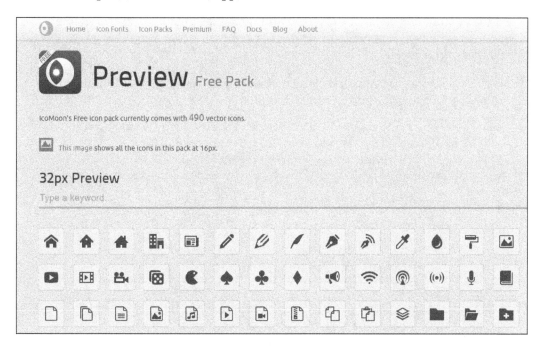

We are simply going to select the ones we need – since they are social media, they are easy to find and free to use – and then we click on the **Generate Font** button at the lower-right of the page, which will generate this page:

We'll then click in the same spot and hit the **Download** button, downloading a zipped file.

We'll then extract the `.eot`, `.woff`, `.svg` and `.ttf` files in another folder, namely `icomoon` or whichever name you prefer. This `icomoon` folder should be placed in the root folder of our project.

Taking a look at the downloaded elements, we'll add the icon classes in the downloaded CSS to our unordered list, like this:

```html
<li class="icon-facebook"><a href="#">Facebook</a></li>
<li class="icon-twitter"><a href="#">Twitter</a></li>
<li class="icon-behance"><a href="#">Behance</a></li>
<li class="icon-dribbble"><a href="#">Dribbble</a></li>
```

Now we'll import the font using CSS in our `Style.scss` file:

```scss
@font-face {
    font-family: 'icomoon';
    src:url('icomoon/icomoon.eot');
    src:url('icomoon/icomoon.eot?#iefix') format('embedded-
      opentype'),
        url('icomoon/icomoon.woff') format('woff'),
        url('icomoon/icomoon.ttf') format('truetype'),
        url('icomoon/icomoon.svg#icomoon') format('svg');
    font-weight: normal;
    font-style: normal;
}
```

Now we'll copy-paste the style for each icon from the downloaded CSS:

```scss
.icon-facebook:before,
.icon-twitter:before,
.icon-behance:before,
.icon-dribbble:before {
    font-family: 'icomoon';
    speak: none;
    font-style: normal;
    font-weight: normal;
    line-height: 1;
    -webkit-font-smoothing: antialiased;
}
.icon-facebook:before {
    content: "\e900";
}
.icon-twitter:before {
```

```
        content: "\e901";
    }
    .icon-dribbble:before {
        content: "\e902";
    }
    .icon-behance:before {
        content: "\e903";
    }
```

Of course, IcoMoon already generated the above for us, we had to transform it into Sass compiling, along with the addition of common and uncommon styles.

Now we're going to style each icon to its coloring and style, starting with some space and alignment, also using the center-align with the negative margins technique:

```
.social {
    margin:2em 0;
    font-family: Helvetica, Arial, sans-serif;

    li {
        position: relative;
        display: inline-block;
        margin: .5em;
        transition :all .15s ease;

        &:hover {
            scale: 1.25;
            color: white;
        }

        &:before {
            position: absolute;
            width: 2em;
            margin-left: -1em;
            top: 1.5em;
            left: 50%;
        }

        a {
            display: block;
            color: inherit;
            padding: 2.5em 1em 1em;
            width: 6em;

            overflow: hidden;
```

```
        white-space: nowrap;
        text-overflow: ellipsis;
      }
    }
  }
```

The preceding code will result in the following:

We'll now only need to inject some color in the newly spaced icons, according to their brands:

```
/* Twitter */
.icon-twitter {color: #00a0d1}
.icon-twitter:hover {background:#00a0d1}
/* Facebook */
.icon-facebook {color: #3b5998}
.icon-facebook:hover {background: #3b5998}
/* Dribbble */
.icon-dribbble {color: #ea4c89}
.icon-dribbble:hover {background: #ea4c89}
/* Behance */
.icon-behance {color: #1769ff}
.icon-behance:hover {background: #1769ff}
```

And that's it!

Now you have a responsive, one-page website built with JSON, scalable fonts, Google Web Fonts, and a scrolling carousel using only natively supported CSS – all of the above built using a Sass preprocessor, which will allow us, for example, to use every color as a variable and call it later very simply.

For the next trick, I'm going to gift you with the Sass code I use as base for typography scaling. It will be easy for you to understand and use it with your values for all your following projects.

Modular typography scale with Sass

The first thing is to set some variables, as it's almost always the same step for every Sass project:

```
$font-size:16px;
$scale:.75;
```

I personally like the fourth ratio, so I'll use it here as an example. As you'll see, it will be easy for you to change it to your preferred one.

We'll now do some math – or better than that, we're going to let Sass do the math for us:

```
$s: $font-size*$scale;
$r: $font-size;
$l: $r/$scale;
$xl: $l/$scale;
$xxl: $xl/$scale;
$xxxl: $xxl/$scale;
```

I personally labeled the base font as Regular, you can name it as you please – and the following sizes are made by simple multiplication/division for our scale factor.

Using the 16px base we're going to obtain the following values:

12, 16, 21, 28, 37, 50, 67

Yes, the H1, for example, is too big – but it doesn't really matter right now, you'll be able to change it in a heartbeat.

Now, how can you use it?

Simple enough, you just have to do one simple declaration – or more, based on the number of variables you need:

```
h1 {
    font-size:$xxxl;
}
```

This will make your CSS look like this:

```
h1 {
   font-size: 50.5679px;
}
```

See the usefulness? Naming the variables as you want, applying another variable for line height and recalling it later is easier than before – and you can apply the values automatically with ems, rems and pixel units as you want – to any property you want with the simple memory of a basic name like small, large, and so on – without having to input any unrelated value ever!

If you're not happy – wait 'til I reveal the next step in our chapter.

Sass Mixin for easy responsiveness

While in the above steps I detailed and attached a quick, fast modular scale with Sass – I'm going to gift you with an easy Mixin for typography so it becomes real-time responsive, enlarging it, and becoming increasingly small while you manage the width of your browser.

The first thing is defining our breakpoint variables: I'm just using random values, feel free to change them as you like:

```
$breakpoints: (
   'large'  : ( max-width: 600px ),
   'medium' : ( max-width: 400px ),
   'small'  : ( max-width: 300px )
);
```

Then I'm declaring a font size value, a Golden Ratio scale and a line height-value (which I almost always forget to set, but I truly love the look and feel it gives to type):

```
@mixin type-size($sizeValue: 1.6, $lineHeight: $sizeValue) {
   font-size: ($sizeValue * 10) + px;
   font-size: ($sizeValue / 1.6) + rem;
   line-height: ($lineHeight * 10) + px;
   line-height: ($lineHeight / 1.6) + rem;
}
```

Then I'm going to declare the mixin that will make the magic - $rate is the amount by which the size and line-height should decrease or increase:

```
@mixin scale-type-linear($fontSize, $lineHeight, $rate) {
  $ratio: $lineHeight/$fontSize;
```

It now returns the initial values for type size and line height:

```
@include type-size($fontSize, $lineHeight);
```

Then it loops through every breakpoint and returns the font and line-height size for each of them:

```
@each $name, $breakpoint in $breakpoints {
  $newFontSize: $fontSize - $rate;
  @media only screen and #{inspect(map-get($breakpoints,
  $name))} {
    @include type-size($newFontSize, $newFontSize*$ratio)
  }
  // Increment our $rate
  $rate: $rate + $rate;
}
}
```

After these steps, it's time for us to code a mixin for our breakpoints – after all, the above would be useless without this step and declaration:

```
@mixin responsive-type-breakpoints($fontSize, $lineHeight, $sizes...)
{
  $ratio: $lineHeight/$fontSize;
  $i: 1;
```

It now returns the initial font size and line-height:

```
@include type-size($fontSize, $lineHeight);
```

The beautiful step: It now loops through each breakpoint and returns the font size and line height for each:

```
@each $name, $breakpoint in $breakpoints {
  @if nth($sizes, $i) != 0 {
  $newFontSize: nth($sizes, $i);
  @media only screen and #{inspect(map-get($breakpoints, $name))}
{
    @include type-size($newFontSize, $newFontSize*$ratio)
  }
  }
  $i: $i + 1;
```

```scss
    }
  }


  //
  @mixin responsive-type-breakpoint($fontSize, $lineHeight, $breakpoint)
  {
    @if (#{inspect(map-get($breakpoints, $breakpoint))}) != 'null' {
      @media only screen and #{inspect(map-get($breakpoints,
  $breakpoint))} {
        @include type-size($fontSize, $lineHeight);
      }
    } @else {
      @media only screen and ($breakpoint) {
        @include type-size($fontSize, $lineHeight);
      }
    }
  }


  .paragraph {
    @include scale-type-linear(3, 3.6, .2);
    @include responsive-type-breakpoints(3, 3.6, 2.4, 2, 1.6);
    @include responsive-type-breakpoints(3, 3.6, 2.4, 0, 1.6);
    @include responsive-type-breakpoint(3, 3.6, 'small');
  }
```

All of the above code will now compile into this:

```css
  .paragraph {
    font-size: 30px;
    font-size: 1.875rem;
    line-height: 36px;
    line-height: 2.25rem; }
    @media only screen and (max-width: 600px) {
      .paragraph {
        font-size: 24px;
        font-size: 1.5rem;
        line-height: 28.8px;
        line-height: 1.8rem; } }
    @media only screen and (max-width: 400px) {
      .paragraph {
        font-size: 20px;
        font-size: 1.25rem;
        line-height: 24px;
        line-height: 1.5rem; } }
```

```
@media only screen and (max-width: 300px) {
  .paragraph {
    font-size: 16px;
    font-size: 1rem;
    line-height: 19.2px;
    line-height: 1.2rem; } }
```

I'm sure you have lots of uses for this mixin. You can also copy-paste it and add other elements that you want generated in the end, like:

```
.h1 {
  @include responsive-type-breakpoint(3, 3.6, 'min-device-width:
800px');
}
```

This will generate the H1 values for the device width of 800px and above.

And in the last step of this chapter which is forthcoming, I will tell you how to generate your own responsive grid with Sass.

A Sass generated responsive grid

We are starting by making a partial Sass file, let's call it `_variables.scss` and start by writing simple variables that will define the number of columns and their max-width, as well as the breakpoints:

```
$grid-columns: 12;
$grid-max-width: 65em;

$breakpoint-small: "only screen and (min-width: 20em)";
$breakpoint-medium: "only screen and (min-width: 30em)";
```

Time to write some mixins, for example for a border-box property which we assume still isn't unified by the various vendors.

And for the sake of this tutorial, we are going to save the mixins in a different file, called `_mixins.scss`.

```
@mixin border-box {
    -webkit-box-sizing: border-box;
    -moz-box-sizing: border-box;
    box-sizing: border-box;
    }
```

Time to really write up the Sass for the Grid, so we create a `grid.scss`.

Our document structure will look like this:

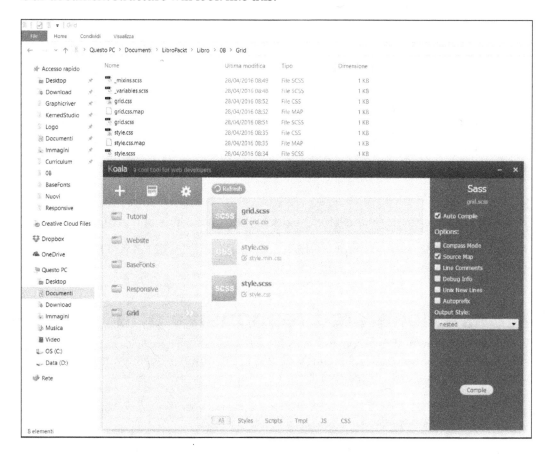

We now import our variables and mixins in the document through the following simple code:

```
@import "variables";
@import "mixins";
```

We start writing by resetting every property:

```
*,
*:after,
*:before {
    margin: 0;
    padding: 0;

    @include border-box;
```

```
        }

%clearfix {
    *zoom: 1;
    &:before,
    &:after {
        content: " ";
        display: table;
    }
    &:after {
        clear: both;
    }
}

.wrapper,
.row {
    @extend %clearfix;
}
```

Which will easily compile in the following CSS:

```
*,
*:after,
*:before {
  margin: 0;
  padding: 0;
  -webkit-box-sizing: border-box;
  -moz-box-sizing: border-box;
  box-sizing: border-box; }

.wrapper,
.row {
  *zoom: 1; }
  .wrapper:before,
  .row:before, .wrapper:after,
  .row:after {
    content: " ";
    display: table; }
  .wrapper:after,
  .row:after {
    clear: both; }
```

We then write a container for our grid:

```
.wrapper {
    width: 95%;
    max-width: $grid-max-width;
    }
```

We write a first breakpoint:

```
@media #{$breakpoint-medium} {
}
```

To make and use the columns, we'll use the Sass loops.

Since the columns, numbers aside, will be the same but for their width, we define a loop that is triggered by the @for instance and will look like this:

```
@for $i from 1 through 12 {

    .column-#{$i} {

        }

}
```

This defines a column class as follows:

```
[class*='column-'] {
    float: left;
    padding: 1em;
    width: 100%;
    min-height: 1px;
    }
width: 100% / $grid-columns * $i;
            }
        }
    }
```

This will execute the loop.

Recalling the column appendix will run this CSS when compiled:

```
.column-1 {

    }

.column-2 {
```

```css
    }

.column-3 {

    }

.column-4 {

    }

.column-5 {

    }

.column-6 {

    }

.column-7 {

    }

.column-8 {

    }

.column-9 {

    }

.column-10 {

    }

.column-11 {

    }

.column-12 {

    }
```

We now only need to obtain values for each of them to define our width defying grid

We can obtain the values with simple math.

Taking the whole (100%) into account, we divide it for the number of desired columns and multiply it for each of the single numbers 'till we line up with the total numbers of columns, like this:

*100 / 12 * 1, 100 / 12 * 2* and so on.

So we put the simple math into the loop, like so:

```
@for $i from 1 through 12 {

    .column-#{$i} {
        width: 100% / 12 * $i;
    }

}
```

This obtains the following:

```
.column-1 {
    width: 8.33333%;
}

.column-2 {
    width: 16.66667%;
}

.column-3 {
    width: 25%;
}

.column-4 {
    width: 33.33333%;
}

.column-5 {
    width: 41.66667%;
}

.column-6 {
```

```
        width: 50%;
    }

    .column-7 {
        width: 58.33333%;
    }

    .column-8 {
        width: 66.66667%;
    }

    .column-9 {
        width: 75%;
    }

    .column-10 {
        width: 83.33333%;
    }

    .column-11 {
        width: 91.66667%;
    }

    .column-12 {
        width: 100%;
    }
```

But what if we want to change the total number of columns? Do we have to manually retrieve and substitute that in each operation?

No; since we are using Sass, we simply change, right now, the number 12 in the loop with the variable `$grid-columns` and that's it!

A magically responsive grid, defined by the number of columns you want each time!

Change just one value and you're good to go!

Summary

Through this long chapter we have been able to see the three content rules you need to achieve one responsive project: meta tag, layout, and media queries, and we've been exploring them to make a responsive, one-page website.

We also looked at how to inject JSON into our projects from a remote API, and how to select and work with custom icon fonts.

We then looked at a ready-to-go modular scale generator built with Sass (a fun little project I know) and how to build a responsive grid for our project using Sass partials and loops.

I bet you have had a ton of fun reading and working your way through this chapter: in the next, final two we'll look into what's coming in the future of responsive typography.

Future Responsive – Hinting

9

After our latest chapter, with a big, code-savvy consideration of the actual state of typography and responsive typography design, it's time we take a look in the ending chapters of this book – at the future state of this technology.

We are going to start with **Hinting** and the actual state of this property for the web.

What is font hinting?

The name refers to one of the properties of typefaces and fonts, in which the latter is adjusted for optimal reading, where Bezier curves are practically moved around to adhere to an underlying grid.

It's a project that started in the late 80's to resolve some rendering conflicts in low resolution printers – which, despite the passage of time, is still as relevant today, just moving the concept from printers to the screen.

The real problem here is that the majority of modern fonts are not designed to behave at the modern screen resolution which is limited in DPI depth – and while more true for the first screens with 72, 96 dpi – it's still true for the 400, and upward, dpi. They were designed to use more than 1500 dpi in the print world.

It's the old Raster versus Vector: Dawn of Rendering battle – where fonts are described as vector-perfect lines and curves – which are then converted to raster pixels on the screen.

Basically every letter gets drawn again at each point size, according to the pixel grid this time – all if not previously seen and done by the typographer – in an automated process by the computer.

Hinting is in fact controlling height, width of the letters, and width of their outlines as well, the angles of the diagonal stems that change every time for a better rendering and so on.

All of the above goes well while I'm typing this book: despite Times New Roman being a free, built-in-every-machine font, it's one of the most time intensive one, since it takes in account everything from hinting and so on – and it has been redesigned over and over for each point size, a tedious and expensive process.

Seriously, it's time to pay Mr. Stanley Morison and his team, and all the unnamed designers which worked on the font, a thank you and tell them how grateful we are.

The four different hinting processes

To start, there are already two different hinting agents: the font itself in the older TrueType system (the `.ttf` font extension) – and the software which reads the font itself in the PostScript format, which explains why modern fonts which are not manually hinted still manage to look crisp and readable in modern times.

There is even a difference from Mac to Windows: the latter takes a pixel-to-pixel approach, aligning any line to the pixel grid, which is why regular weights looks lighter – and bold ones looks heavier than the ones on a Mac screen.

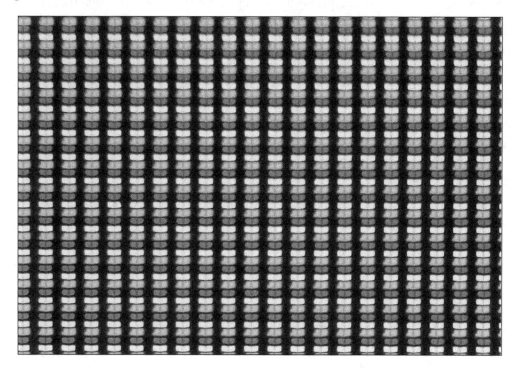

An LCD screen under magnification. Image released under CC,
author unknown – the image shows a pixel grid.

The Mac approach instead, is proprietary built-in software called Quartz, which renders itself at every font despite their origin, making better balanced and readable fonts on everything that it's passed to.

So for this chapter we are going to observe Hinting behavior on a Windows machine, (since we have different possibilities to analyze) in a PostScript format, which is the direction where every type, even on the web, is moving for its rendering solution.

Black and white rendering

Developed when pixels only actually had two states, on/off, it controls which pixels are active or inactive at a certain point size.

Being based on a pixel grid, every piece of the font is heavily modified to fit the grid. Usually white pixels are added by hand to make the font more legible.

Manually hinting a font this way could take, at least, 80 hours and it generated a scaled font, really similar to the 80/90 arcade games screens.

It is now obsolete.

The quick brown fox jumps over the lazy dog.

The quick brown fox jumps over the lazy dog.

Blogger Sans Regular 10 and 15pt with Black & White Hinting at 200% zoom.

Gray-scale rendering

This hinting process takes care of rendering with the antialiasing technique, introduced in Windows 98.

It adds various gray shades between the black and white pixels, so the font renders smoothly.

Manually hinting this way could take up to 72 hours for a single font; the old, bulky monitors of the nineties used it heavily.

The quick brown fox jumps over the lazy dog.

The quick brown fox jumps over the lazy dog.

 Blogger Sans Regular 10 and 15pt with Gray-scale Hinting at 200% zoom.

ClearType rendering

This makes use of hinting only horizontally, not vertically – and it's a Microsoft proprietary technology. It simulates the three colors of the single pixel to achieve smoother results.

Taking care only of horizontal rendering means that scaling the text horizontally can look sharper up to three times the original size – and it also reduces by half, the time to develop a font: a single font with this technique takes up to 40 hours.

The quick brown fox jumps over the lazy dog.

The quick brown fox jumps over the lazy dog.

 Blogger Sans Regular 10 and 15pt with ClearType hinting at 200% zoom.

DirectWrite rendering

This came out first with Windows 7, it is an advancement of ClearType but with added sub-pixel vertical hinting.

Subpixel rendering takes into account the fact that the physical pixel on the screen is actually made of three RGB colored pixels – and while they aren't directly visible to the human eye, their change in color can be perceived, hence increasing the physical pixel resolution. More on subpixel rendering can be found on Wikipedia:

```
https://en.wikipedia.org/wiki/Subpixel_rendering
```

This means that the curves are smoother – and it improves rendering of OpenType too – but it also doubles hinting time, which done manually can be back at 70 or more hours per font. It began its utilization with Internet Explorer 9.

The quick brown fox jumps over the lazy dog.

The quick brown fox jumps over the lazy dog.

 Blogger Sans Regular 10 and 15pt with DirectWrite hinting at 200% zoom

Difficulties for type designers – and hinting's future

All of the above means a more manual, tedious application for every font designer out there – and it also means that the output won't always be the desired one, since there are varieties and different platforms.

Manual hinting, to be cross compatible through various sources, would take ages for each and every font, something that I really hope no one would consider, unless it's a project very well paid.

This also bring problems with the new era of online typography rendering – even if the concepts above describe responsive typography long before our current days, since it allows the font to answer to the different resolutions and conditions – prior to online layouts.

One of the solutions for hinting on the Web which is kind of pushed right now is a sort of Macro cleaver hinting.

Called through specific media queries, it would allow special features to be called by:

- Ascenders and descenders that shrink with a reduction of line-height
- Glyphs that condense – both automatically or referring to a pre-existing condensed typeface – when the width of their container is reduced
- Subtle weight adjustment in the same font file without calling other external ones

While a joy for a web developer to hear and express such sentiments and requests, the solution would be impractical for type designers as it will add to the already long time of designing a font – it is a non-standard way which will take years to be standard and probably end up being surpassed – rather than the previous way of designing fonts.

 If you're not a professional type designer that won't mean a lot to you – you'll just move two or three points down an existing letter and call it a day.

But for professional people this would mean having to recalculate curves, straight lines, widths of every weight, and hinting for each change – something that everyone that has been through in regards to font design development, won't even come near to thinking about.

Another problem with pixel densities

As of today, as said, we live in a world with growing and shrinking screen sizes with no standards – and the smaller screens are having a blast in screen density.

While this is a welcome change, it also brings a new problem on the table with rendering itself. While the majority of smartphones now offer higher density, a vast majority of tablets and laptops don't do this. And it's all down to the viewport width.

Let me explain it better: let's consider the Asus Zenbook Prime. A 13.3 screen version come with a 1920x1080 pixel resolution, which in depth is 168dpi. A 11.1 version has the very same resolution, which works out at 189dpi.

Web type at 16pt, rendered in standard non-high pixel density, render in a 1x manner, with true 16 pixels per character (and it's the same rendering in most of last year's laptops that sport a varying 96-115 depth range).

So, on one of the standard displays, a 16px renders at a physical 0.14 inches, around 10pts, a decent size for reading.

But on one of the two Zenbooks, the same text is just 0.09 inches high – 49% smaller.

See where the problem is? Same resolution, different results.

Bacon ipsum dolor amet filet mignon swine pork loin, strip steak cupim drumstick landjaeger pork sausage brisket cow. Turkey rump tail chicken frankfurter, hamburger sirloin ham landjaeger beef ribs flank. Bresaola tenderloin pork chop landjaeger biltong, short ribs cow pastrami kevin ground round. Tenderloin flank ham pig pork chop shankle. Beef ribs fatback picanha cupim. Chicken kevin alcatra, pork loin beef ribs doner tail corned beef drumstick fatback strip steak pig.

Bacon ipsum dolor amet filet mignon swine pork loin, strip steak cupim drumstick landjaeger pork sausage brisket cow. Turkey rump tail chicken frankfurter, hamburger sirloin ham landjaeger beef ribs flank. Bresaola tenderloin pork chop landjaeger biltong, short ribs cow pastrami kevin ground round. Tenderloin flank ham pig pork chop shankle. Beef ribs fatback picanha cupim. Chicken kevin alcatra, pork loin beef ribs doner tail corned beef drumstick fatback strip steak pig

That's a difference – especially considering the resolution is the same with my laptop used for the production of the image and the Zenbook, the same 1920x1080 pixels.

Some machines, such as Windows 7 for example – which the above Zenbooks run on – don't allow the high density display to work according to their standard, thus making the above, theoretical solution, a problem.

Can you imagine shrinking the line height and the ascenders/descenders for the right provided example?

My solution for hinting on the Web

While, luckily, due to the current, always-evolving, depth of modern – even mobile – screens, the problem of hinting is vanishing, it will be a long time 'til this happens, so foremost, there must be an implementation of a theoretical solution.

Personally speaking, since hinting has been developed and implemented for almost 30 years as of today, I don't see the addition of other features like shrinking ascenders and descenders as an acceptable solution.

But I certainly see calling hinting as a variable in media queries an awesome solution. Of course, we are far from this being implemented, since we are still far from the standardization of `.woff` in web design as the official Web Format Font.

Since thousands of typefaces already implement hinting in one form or another – and since the movement to a 16px based web, I don't think we'll be needing hinting for much longer – at least for the web.

What I see as a solution is the standardization of a type of hinting for the web, as a media query that can be called by the web developer easily, in two or three forms to add the necessary legibility – as a border.

For example, see the following:

```
@media
(-webkit-min-device-pixel-ratio: 2), (min-resolution: 192dpi) {
Font-hinting: small
```

(Of course the `font-hinting` property is invented for the sake of this example and idea by me.)

The above snippet will make the addition of what is perceived by the designer for a font to be small format – of a border-like pixel addition following the current font grid (easily done since a vector standard font format will be used) of, let's say two pixels.

Yes, it will make the font seem a little bolder than usual on lighter fonts for example, but the shape won't be lost since it's a vector file – and the appearance and readability will be saved.

Instead, type the following:

```
Font-hinting: large
```

This will make the removal – of 1 or 2 pixels from the same text, where a web developer or designer will consider the text on the screen to be big/large in appearance – both based on the font or the viewport width.

The type will seem a little lighter, but since the larger type will be seen onscreen with a high number of pixel density, we won't even notice it.

Of course, everything will have to be standard – as the number of exact pixels to be removed or added, to be called through an additional query, as for example:

```
Hinting-remove: 2px;
```

Doing so will allow typographers to keep working the way they have done for almost 30 years – with the simple addition of one or two media queries for the developer/designer to remember – and the addition of one new way to be remembered by browser software developers.

Or if the coding of a media query for something that we all hope is set to vanish anytime soon (the same about hinting has been said for 20 years) is too much and I completely understand it, the developer can write code such as the following:

```
@media only screen and (-webkit-min-device-pixel-ratio: 1.5),
       only screen and (-o-min-device-pixel-ratio: '150/100'),
       only screen and (min-resolution: 96dpi),
       only screen and (min-resolution: 1.5dppx) {
    font-weight: 300;
}
```

This will simply allow high density screens to use a lighter, well rendered weight – and to use a bolder one on a smaller screen.

Or just adjusting the size like this will also work:

```
body {
  font-size: 100%;
}

@media screen and (min-width: 1200px) {
  body {
    font-size: 125%;
  }
}
```

To my mind, making the solution automatically work based on machines is not a solution – Windows 7 doesn't allow HI-DPI display to work correctly, rendering the text on 1x. Why is the machine left to do the guessing, if it can't even work correctly in the first place? I trust an experienced web designer or developer to make the call with the correct sized media queries, whether to implement a hinting solution through one simple line of code or not.

Summary

In this chapter we learnt everything about hinting. How it's been implemented, and why it's been useful. We also saw two theoretical ways of approaching it within the responsive web.

In the next and last chapter, we'll see how to manipulate the text layout with CSS3 properties.

10
Future Responsive – Drop Caps and Shapes

In our latest chapter, we are going to analyze two useful figures for our online typography, drop caps and shapes, and their future development.

What drop caps are and how to use them

Drop caps are the large letter you see in handmade books from centuries ago.

They have been in use for thousands of years, as they increased readability and legibility by marking specific passages and guiding the reader's eye through the text.

They also are beautiful. So why aren't they more used throughout the web?

Their appearance on the screen is different from system to system and they can be a little tedious to be measured and put in – but I'll guide you through easy methods to make use of the drop caps whenever you want.

This P is Historiated, since it contains a picture of a specific person or story. And it's illuminated, since its gold decorations represent the light of God.

They were also used to portray the use of alphabetical order.

Today, with industrialization, drop caps aren't a reading necessity – they are only used as decorative elements, often to communicate old or traditional feelings.

There are four different methods to make a drop cap on the web and I'm going to illustrate each of them for you.

Drop cap with an image

If you want a drop cap with maximum consistency across all operating systems and screens, your best bet is to use an image.

It is obtained with a simple class as shown following:

```
<p><span class="drop L">L</span>orem Ipsum sit dolor … </p>
```

You may notice that I used two classes for one single letter. Doing so allowed me to style the space using the drop class:

```
.drop{
    display:block;
    float:left;
    width:100px;
    height:112px;
    margin-top:5px;
    padding-right:8px;
    text-indent: 100%;
    white-space: nowrap;
    overflow: hidden;
}
```

And a class letter to aim at the letter image.

```
.L{
    background: url(L_small.jpg) 0 0 no-repeat;
}
```

The code will now result in something like this, a web ready and safe drop cap.

[187]

Letter over an image

It's time for our second method, writing our letter over an image. This time we are going to use the same background for each and every letter, so only one class of the background will be needed.

```
<p><span class="cap">L</span>orem Ipsum sit dolor … </p>

.cap{
    display:block;
    float:left;
    width:72px;
    height:52px;
    font-size: 400%;
    color:#ffffff;
    margin-top:5px;
    padding-top:20px;
    margin-right:8px;
    text-align:center;
    background: url(back.jpg) 0 0 no-repeat;
    }
```

You should now obtain something like this:

 orem Ipsum is simply dummy text of the printing and typesetting industry. Lorem Ipsum has been the industry's standard dummy text ever since the 1500s, when an unknown printer took a galley of type and scrambled it to make a type specimen book. It has survived not only five centuries, but also the leap into electronic typesetting, remaining essentially unchanged. It was popularised in the 1960s with the release of Letraset sheets containing Lorem Ipsum passages, and more recently with desktop publishing software like Aldus PageMaker including versions of Lorem Ipsum.

Creating a class with no image

Back to what I love more, pure text. It's a very confident, bold result that stays true in the vast majority of browsers, so it can be used immediately – and it's achieved with a single class:

```
<p><span class="dropcap">L</span>orem Ipsum sit dolor … </p>

.dropcap{
    float:left;
    font-size:400%;
    margin-top:14px;
    margin-right:5px;
    color:#8C8273;
    }
```

With this simple code you'll achieve something like this:

orem Ipsum is simply dummy text of the printing and typesetting industry. Lorem Ipsum has been the industry's standard dummy text ever since the 1500s, when an unknown printer took a galley of type and scrambled it to make a type specimen book. It has survived not only five centuries, but also the leap into electronic typesetting, remaining essentially unchanged. It was popularised in the 1960s with the release of Letraset sheets containing Lorem Ipsum passages, and more recently with desktop publishing software like Aldus PageMaker including versions of Lorem Ipsum.

Drop caps with pseudo-elements

It's time for my beloved solution, using CSS3 pseudo-elements with no addition of classes (I just added a section element to target only the desired piece in my demo code)

Use the following code:

```
section p:first-child:first-letter{
    float:left;
    font-size:400%;
    margin-top:7px;
    margin-right:5px;
    color:#992E00;
    }
```

This will target only the paragraph within a section and show this in the browser:

orem Ipsum is simply dummy text of the printing and typesetting industry. Lorem Ipsum has been the industry's standard dummy text ever since the 1500s, when an unknown printer took a galley of type and scrambled it to make a type specimen book. It has survived not only five centuries, but also the leap into electronic typesetting, remaining essentially unchanged. It was popularised in the 1960s with the release of Letraset sheets containing Lorem Ipsum passages, and more recently with desktop publishing software like Aldus PageMaker including versions of Lorem Ipsum.

All of the above solutions as of today are stylistically valid and cross-browser compatible, they won't show or create much of a problem in the majority of software – and you'll be able to better illustrate your text online.

Just remember that beautiful, balanced drop caps require time and effort, both in styling and aligning them correctly.

Making it responsive in each case requires alternating the image width, keeping height auto in our media queries – or simply altering the font report where no image is used.

Onto the future – Shaping your text

All we did till now was beautiful text, well paired and calculated. But what if we want to break the old squared development and present our text inside a wide array of shapes?

Luckily, with the newly-introduced CSS3 shape element (which is still much unsupported) we can do it!

I will guide you through this, it will just be a little bit since we'll be able to fully use it in our day-by-day projects. Combined with clipping and masking, CSS filters, compositing, and blending we'll be able to make the web our playground more than ever. But it's time for us to focus on our typography.

You can apply a shape to an element on the page by attaching one of its properties, since the shapes right now are functions:

```
Element {
Shape-outside: polygon(parameters);
}
```

The currently existing functions are:

- Circle
- Ellipse
- Inset
- Polygon

Each of them is defined by a set of points. The properties instead are:

- `Shape-outside` (wrap content around a shape)
- `Shape-inside` (wrap its content inside the given shape)

You can use the `shape-margin` property to lay a margin between your shape and your text. The inside shape instead answers to the `shape-padding` property.

Right now only two rules are needed for shapes to be rendered: the element must be floated, and it must have dimensions, since those will be the starting point to establish a coordinate system.

For example, see the following code:

```
.element {
    float: left;
    height: 10em;
    width: 15em;
    shape-outside: circle();
}
```

This will tell our browser to draw a 15em circle around our element.

Each shape is defined and created inside a reference box to define its extents – taking in account not only the given object dimension but also its margins, paddings and borders.

For example:

```
shape-outside: circle(250px at 50% 50%) padding-box;
```

This will define a circular space of 250px size in the middle of our element until it touches the padding box, it won't go further than that.

A shape tutorial

We are going to make a simple bio section for a fictional website.

Right now we simply added a small profile image – and a bio inside a p

This is the current CSS:

```
img   { width: 150px;
    float: left;
    height: auto;
    border-radius: 50%;
    margin-right: 15px;
}

p {max-width: 30%;
}
```

This is what we have thus far, with the text outlining the shape as a simple square:

Lorem Ipsum is simply dummy text of the printing and typesetting industry. Lorem Ipsum has been the industry's standard dummy text ever since the 1500s, when an unknown printer took a galley of type and scrambled it to make a type specimen book. It has survived not only five centuries, but also the leap into electronic typesetting, remaining essentially unchanged. It was popularised in the 1960s with the release of Letraset sheets containing Lorem Ipsum passages, and more recently with desktop publishing software like Aldus PageMaker including versions of Lorem Ipsum.

It's now time to integrate the shape into our image to make the text flow, all below inside the `img` element:

```
shape-outside: circle();
shape-margin: 15px;
}
```

With this code, the browser will render a 15px circle around our image element and the text will change its flow accordingly:

Lorem Ipsum is simply dummy text of the printing and typesetting industry. Lorem Ipsum has been the industry's standard dummy text ever since the 1500s, when an unknown printer took a galley of type and scrambled it to make a type specimen book. It has survived not only five centuries, but also the leap into electronic typesetting, remaining essentially unchanged. It was popularised in the 1960s with the release of Letraset sheets containing Lorem Ipsum passages, and more recently with desktop publishing software like Aldus PageMaker including versions of Lorem Ipsum.

Isn't it extraordinary?!?

Other parameters to know about shapes right now are:

- The parameters inside the function for the circle are its radius and the starting position.
- Closest-side and furthest-side are two valid variables, with closest being the browser base, meaning the radius will be taken as the length from the center to the closer side. For example:
    - shape-outside: circle(farthest-side at 25% 25%); defines a circle whose radius is half the length of the longest side, positioned at the point of coordinates 25% 25% on the element's coordinate system
    - shape-inside: circle(250px at 500px 300px); /* defines a circle whose center is positioned at 500px horizontally and 300px vertically, with a radius of 250px */
- The ellipse function works the same way but it takes two variables: one for the *x*-radius and one for the *y*-radius.
- Inset is created to make rectangular shapes inside our initial rectangle, but since the web is already rectangular, we can use it for another thing: making rounded angles rectangular with content flowing around those shapes, since it takes two options: a parameter for the inner injection of the object and a second value for the roundness of its corners.
- Polygon is the last element available, in which you can create which shape you want with coordinates given by pairs, each one specifying the position of one point.

Defining a shape using an image

To let our text flow automatically around a given image, the image itself should have an alpha channel.

Calling an object as a path is easy:

```
.leaf-shaped-element {
    float: left;
    width: 400px;
    height: 400px;
    shape-outside: url(leaf.png);
    shape-margin: 15px;
}
```

You just pinpoint the URL to the image and you're done! (I left my leaf image in the tutorial files for you to experiment with)

Also you can use the shape-image-threshold property for images with an alpha channel: Setting it to 0.6 value for example will mean that the shape will take into account pixels that are more than 60% opaque.

Values range from 0.0 – completely transparent – to 1.0, completely opaque.

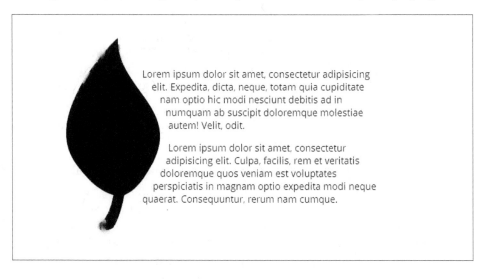

CSS shapes in responsive web design

How does all the above fit in to our responsive web design?

Everything in shapes-outside can be set using relative or percentage units, even the shapes – so everything can be scaled accordingly to our viewpoint.

Shape-inside instead is still unresponsive – its responsiveness will be pushed by the W3C as soon as possible.

In the future

Right now, CSS shapes are cut out from the largest CSS3 spec – in the future, when they are finally standardized, we'll see the rise of CSS exclusions as well, which will allow us to wrap content around non floated elements, allowing the entire shape to be wrapped on every side, for example, on absolutely positioned elements.

Summary

Within this short, but knowledge-filled chapter we managed to encounter drop caps and shapes, what they both are, and how to introduce them to our daily workflow using simple, semantic code.

This also concludes our book – I hope you had as much fun reading and learning together as I had teaching and writing this book for you, dear reader.

So don't stop exploring and trying new things, the future is just around the corner.

To our success,

Dario Calonaci

Index

www.ingramcontent.com/pod-product-compliance
Lightning Source LLC
LaVergne TN
LVHW081341050326
832903LV00024B/1244